THE BOOK OF WISDOM

THE AGE OF MINDFULNESS

REGINALD O'NEAL GIBSON

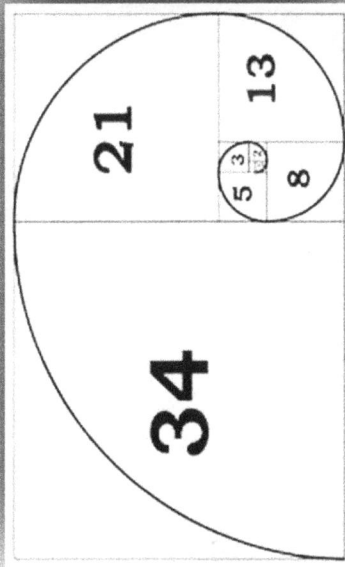

REGINALD O'NEAL GIBSON

REGINALD O'NEAL GIBSON

Copyright © 2017 Reginald Gibson

ISBN-13: 9780692988626

Printed in the United States

DEDICATION

This book is dedicated for those who seek but often find it difficult to navigate through the various distractions within our daily routines. The sensational ways of vague worldly suggestions prevents one's understandings of the natural laws of life. I seek to help clarify these false perceptions, in part distorting the proper use and faculties of the mind. In this book I speak of the law of attraction, mindfulness, consciousness, enlightenment and abundance but only by way of the original teachings. There are many forms of good content on the matter of right from wrong but please beware of misleading content, opinions and ideas crafted to blind the masses from their created purposes. In this, know the content of this book is derived from the teachings of Jesus Christ, the King James Bible and my personal hardships throughout life; successfully overcame with the assistance of the Holy Spirit. I willingly submit this spiritually acquired knowledge, for the purposes of confirming "we all have unimaginable power embedded within our mental storehouse". God bless, as we usher in the presence of his wisdom, mercy and favor over our lives.

Prologue

The BOOK of WISDOM: the Age of Mindfulness, con-
tains thirteen chapters regarding the everyday challenges
within our modern lifestyles. This book pours from the
humble conviction of my spirit to bring light to the darkness of the un-clarified mind. Seeking that which has been
bestowed within our hearts upon creation, is of great demand in a generation of scarified knowledge. What better
way for I, being a servant of God, to lead by way of the
Holy Spirit, as an example of his and her intended purposes for all of mankind. Humbly I submit onto you the fluidity of spiritual understandings, This in absolute faith that
you'll unveil the truth in God's purpose for your life. This
in the simplistic insight of everyday challenges, I offer you
through the transparency of my humility, how to interact
and surpass the wicked intentions of the opposer. Such a
humble book, challenging the pseudo greatness of man's
overwhelming submissiveness to self idolization. This is to
the likeness of David and Goliath, Moses and Ramses and
to a lesser extent, author against the strongholds and principalities of the world. This book will guide upon the footsteps of your journey, how to reveal wisdom within your
spirit, provide clarity within the depths of your mind and
abundance within your heart. This unto you, I render the
BOOK of WISDOM: the Age of Mindfulness within the
"fear of God," as the key to my life's work; please enjoy.

THE BOOK OF WISDOM

REGINALD O'NEAL GIBSON

CONTENTS i

1 THE LIFE OF LIFE — Pg. 13
2 THE FIRT KEY STEPS — Pg. 20
3 FOCUS YOUR POWER — Pg. 28
4 YOUR JOURNEY YOUR LEGACY — Pg. 37
5 SHAME, SHAME; JUDGE NOT — Pg. 47
6 THE LIKENESS OF LOVE — Pg. 64
7 THE THREE ROUTES — Pg. 76
8 NO OPINIONS NECESSARY — Pg. 83
9 KNOW THY SELF — Pg. 94
10 COMMUNION OF THE RIGHT-EOUS — Pg. 103
11 ENTER THE TRUTH — Pg. 133
12 BALANCE OF MIND — Pg. 147
13 MASTERY OF THOUGHT — Pg. 158

10

ACKNOWLEDGMENTS

I would like to express my thanks and appreciation for the trials that inspired me to overcome the problematic circumstances set within life. This is not to exclude those who once would be considered enemies, nay-sayers and false-friends cloaked in deceptive ways. Thank you as well and please forgive me of my past adolescent and judgmental blunders concerning your opinions over my calling. I openly forgive and solute those thought to be of an offending nature, being they were an intricate part in God's overall purpose for my life. Know that we're not all meant to be physically alike or in agreement on trivial matters of personal concerns but "we are as one" within the unfathomable wisdom of the Holy Spirit. Know that I love you and for any bitter thoughts or words against myself or my purpose, I pray for the healing, growth and proper guidance for us all. Again, I pray in the mighty name of Jesus, please forgive us of our sins and any misunderstandings that could otherwise lead us into the misguided ways of harden hearts. May God bless your journey.

REGINALD O'NEAL GIBSON

1 CHAPTER

LIFE OF LIFE

Hey, how's it going? Life that is, how is life or your perception of life going for you? I hope all is well. Also, it is my hope and prayer that you can see life for the beauty and purpose it has to offer and the same for it's meaning within the experience.

Recently, I've taken some time to meditate, pray and rest in the teachings and wisdom of Christ, the result was simply amazing. I came to the conclusion that my perceptions of life was slightly diverted by the distractions of mostly "fear based" propaganda.

Like many, I became clouded with opinions rather than the simple truth in things. Only issue was, things or the circumstances of things which happens in life are the direct results of our actions or perceptions thereof.

In other words, we manifest problems, issues or uncomfortable circumstances because we lose or become diverted from the understandings of the natural laws of life; which are simplistic at best.

Life is simply life, its purpose happens to be completely unaffected by the "little things" we create along our journey. Here's what I'm getting at, find out who you are through the teachings of Christ.

Find out what spiritual gifts you were given within the womb and make it your life mission to become that person.

In this your life will change for the better, your outlook, your ideas and your purpose; why? Because just as life is life, you would have found the meaning of you, and in this meaning, nothing in life as a distraction can take you off course from your created purpose.

Here's a notable mention that will save you from a life of strife and pointless denial, the search of mindfulness is utterly useless if the mind is cluttered with confusion.

In other words, how can you find yourself in the darkness of an unenlightened mindset. This is why I insist on the teachings of Christ, learn this and you'll learn yourself. When this is accomplished, you can find true mindfulness; that is the mindfulness in Christ. So again, I ask you Hey, how is life going?

Now let's slow down a bit, I've got another question to ask. Where are you headed or better yet, where would you like to go? Let's be honest, if you're like most you have big dreams and ideas but may not actually know how to get there.

Not to worry, in fact it's the "worrying" part that prevents most people from taking the steps to achieve their higher goals and personal achievements.

Once again, may I suggest just get over what others may think about your current situation, ignore your fears and boldly take that first important step.

Now that you're equipped, claim your victory, claim your purpose and most of all, while the momentum is in your favor, please commit to the follow-through; one confident step at a time!

This simple method will allow an overflow of timeless knowledge, that is if you're really committed to reaching that goal or place of personal achievement. All it takes is as mentioned, one foot in front of the other but allow me to paint a picture to explain the right way to take this leap of faith.

Let's take a closer look at the "one step in front of the other" analogy. Please know to take the steps in sequence you first must be in accordance with the other. This is the representation of your mind and spirit working together to motivate your body to reposition itself for the favor of God.

This is why it's imperative to repent and lay to rest your own vices first! If you truly want abundance, health, wealth and all the blessings bestowed in life for your purpose, you must obtain the ear for wisdom.

In other words to hear the words of the Holy Spirit and allow it to guide your life, you must quiet the mind.

This is done by leaving the loudness of your guilt behind, your boisterous thoughts of anger and that gossiping un-forgiving seed nurtured by the pain of people who have offended you.

Peace be still in your temple, become deaf to the mind chatter of the world and just listen. What is sought from wisdom, will soon echo from the hidden chambers of your heart; aligning once again the connection between mind, body and soul.

In other words, to properly align yourself with forward motion of any kind, you must connect or come into agreement with like minded counterparts.

That is a counterpart that conducive to the physical and spiritual; just commit yourself to make that push forward. Getting back to the example of the foot, understand the action of the foot isn't to coordinate with the ear, shoulder or chin but rather the adjacent other foot.

So may I advise, when you start taking your steps to achievement of personal goals, don't waste time soliciting the advice from people who are not interested in the direc-tion you're heading. Especially if people care less for your vision, ideas or interests, why waste the time.

This also applies to the people we desire to be involved, I'm talking close family members, old friends, business partners and yes even your spouse!

Keep in mind, upon the journey of finding your mindfulness in christ, your purpose may not fit with the mindset of others nearest you.

In the likelihood of this, love them anyway but make the time to do the work God created you to do.

Quick note, don't confuse your job i.e. the company you clock in for a paycheck or compensation, with the purposeful "work" God created in you to encompass as your life's purpose.

If you find this even the slightest bit confusing, simply look up the definitions between job and work and you'll quickly understand that one, is of man's purpose and the other our heavenly father's.

As a matter of fact, in appreciation of reading this book, I'd consider it my privilege to at least provide a paraphrase of the definitions for your convenience but as good practice, always confirm any information shared, given or taught. Which is why I recommend the best selling book of all times, the Holy Bible.

In this will be your complete guide but for the purposes of this book, consider it "a step" in the right direction. Know that one of my purposes or "work" is to provide a "in time correlation" of how the wisdom of the bible still resonates in today's society.

So, regarding the meaning of the word "job," it defines as compensation for employment of services rendered to a business, company or establishment for an agreed service.

Defining the word "work" goes as follows, the physical or mental calling of achievement through the effort and activity by way of purposeful result for yourself or others.

In short you clock in to get something back, you work to accomplish something vastly more meaningful to life. For instance you 'workout' to stay in shape, you 'work-through' issues that are in your way and you 'work towards' building a meaningful relationship. Finding out what your life's work is, will ultimately be revealed as you progress through the steps towards mental clarity.

Furthermore, discovering your embedded gifts, resources and connections to achieve what you're destined to become, starts with mind-dumping the clutter impairing your thought processes. Keep in mind you can always seek out an honest mentor, enroll in a like minded class, find a good bible based church and even go on a spiritual pilgrimage. Lastly, at the minimum you owe it to yourself to diligently research, research and research!

Faithfully the next few paragraphs may help, giving you a shoulder view of the mindset I had when faced with certain possibly life changing barriers.

More specifically, those certain types of barriers that develop into ultimatums or problematic cliffhangers threatening to divert your climb towards that higher lifestyle. Just remember, change starts in the mind of the one who honestly seeks the path of their created purposes.

In this you should know when to boldly take a chance embracing that ever-fearful leap of faith. Once achieved, gather your sources, find yourself in Christ and let the journey begin!

Genesis 2:7

"And the LORD God formed man of the dust of the ground, and breathed into his nostrils the breath of life; and man became a living soul."

-King James Bible

2 CHAPTER

THE FIRST KEY STEP

Like many, at times we often find ourselves feeling separate from the crowd. A sense that soon contributes to a distant place in thought, seeking out the comfort of one's solidarity. Often the mere grip of this feeling can easily pull a person into sensationalism, creating what is believed to be that of sound mind and body.

Ideas and opinions that appear to be appropriate to personal beliefs and acquired teachings are eagerly accepted as a norm. This is why most are swift to judgement, fueling the perceived images of the powers that be, the people within their environment and even unassuming family members and friends.

Before they know it, they'll be spewing their own confusions and fear based off their own worries and presumptions. This is the basis of misinformation, miseducation and the like thereof; better known as distractions.

The purpose of this book is to remind those who seek the underlying truth that speaks to us all but somehow gets muffled in translation. Often brushed off as a gut feeling, intuition or an insecure thought, we all have warning signs assisting our conscious, basically red-flagging our directions in life. The true and most difficult part in understanding this debacle, relies in the first key step.

Moreover, learning that which it takes to overcome our own personal vices, created fears and unmerited assumptions.

So, one of the best ways to divert from the distractions, is to indulge in a thought provoking story to help take your mind off the problematic current affairs; seemingly thriving all around us. Ever wanted to just kick your feet up, relax and watch a movie; same scenario.

Also if you look a little closer, you may find a deeper understanding within the stories but know the true meanings of things always appears after the journey. That is to say after you've experienced the relativity of these stories, notice how similar the trials are to your own personal experiences or maybe someone you know.

Just keep in mind, the only difference between the circumstances and how they unfold affecting your life is the wisdom or lack thereof applied, either before or after the experience. Take some time to enjoy and relate to the goodness within these compilations.

I promise, no matter what level of education or under-standing you may have acquired, the spirit of wisdom will reveal the natural order of God's purpose for your life.

Here's one of my true-life circumstances I had to endure, before becoming enlightened by the Holy Spirit. If diligent in what you seek, you'll uncover the hidden root of this story and the power of its purpose; take a walk with me and please enjoy.

My walk is a walk of purpose, tremendous in the dili-gence of will. This walk is of blessed suffering, filled with burdened, weighed heavily on truth in leadership by exam-ple. Someone has to bare the terrain of a path already trav-eled, bled upon and ultimately sacrificed for our salvation.

Times have changed but the loneliness of being awakened in the midst of the darkest hour; remains steadfast. Some-one must continue, someone trustworthy, someone selfless in the understanding that for no other reason but to push on relentlessly, just because it's a simple must. That is, someone like myself.

So steady is my breath as the arrows strike, ricocheting off the shell of my back. One mindset, one purpose while pressing onward; persisting and ultimately falling forward into my blessed destiny.

Clarity is my vision, with closed eyes to the wiles of deceit; I press on. Onward in the steps of christ as I confirm my purpose in diligence. This insatiable drive, this relentless push is but a fragment of my journey upon the righteous path.

Frozen terrains of trapped water beneath my feet, created from tears of ignorance now desolated and cold from bridges burned. A past far from the hopes of quenching my thirst in closure, for in this spirit I shall not turn back.

Scorched earth as the cracked surface reveals only dust, I will not return to; not just yet.

Tedious to the body but enlightened to the eternal spirit, I carry on, ignoring the laughter of the wicked basking in the lusts of the world.

As I pass through the illusion of time, I lay rest what was thought to be past, as it ignites the fuel to my destined salvation. Overcoming the debris of broken barriers crumbling beneath my feet, awakens the taste of sweet nectar to my senses.

Bitter in the mouths of naysayers, yet curious in their attempt to follow, only to soon lose their way in the complacency of their chosen distractions. Even still my walk must continue, for it is my purpose and within this purpose; I hold a beautiful secret.

Unknown to my surroundings, I desperately hold the blessed memories and prayers of love and kindness from friends and family. Continuously flowing through my heart, their hope is a strength I've use to heal my weathered soul.

One of many reasons why I walk relentlessly onward; towards a destined purpose. The pain of whom thought to be enemies offensive to my physical being and soul is my nourishment as well; pressing me forward in forgiveness of their misguided ways.

It is in this miracle of love that holds the mind together from the distractions of a weighted consciousness.

The struggle to hold onto the spirit within the heart and the enlightenment of the mind is a horrendous battle, fought continuously within the realm of distractions.

But this realm, this reality, and the accepted purpose of our creation, is the walk of life upon the narrow path of salvation.

Lonely in its purpose but traveled by many; in this we have stumbled upon the key to heaven on earth. Know that while on this journey I see you, you are not alone and you are not forgotten. I acknowledge your turmoil as well while on this righteous path.

Thank you for taking part in this walk or better yet glimpse of a much bigger picture, regarding the canvas of life.

Remember, as mentioned "If diligent in what you seek, you'll uncover the hidden root of this story and the power of its purpose."

Even though our ideas, hopes and prayers are often of contrasted vision, I see we're both moving forward, relentlessly in the footsteps of christ likeness. Within this I also see that neither of us is truly alone, even in the midst of the darker times as our focus is fixed on the light of the world.

Thank you for your presence, obviously I acknowledge that it's not all about my purpose in strife but our struggles as the human race to ascend together. So let's continue this path united, one in christ, one in mind, body and spirit. Standing side by side putting one foot in front of the other; one purposely blessed step at a time.

In whatever battles, thought processes or lifestyle choices you're currently going through, the first step is always the most difficult.

In the mindset of a paradigm shift, when you or someone you know faithfully takes that key step, that total leap of faith; take pride and exemplify confidence.

This will bring about a higher vibration of positive return, that is people will notice your exuberance, your zeal for life and ultimately your change on a physical level.

This is what the spirit of wisdom is trying to channel through you, breathe in this moment and you'll become calm within all storms. Be one with this spirit, stand firm in the battle armor gifted and allow what was given as the comforter to lead your footsteps.

This is known as dealing with the enemy from within. Please accept that there are no true enemies around you, only the battle within your mind; created from fear. Guard your mind with relentless valor and allow no one or thing to corrupt your perception.

In this you would have quickly vanquished the wicked intentions of something who seeks destruction by way of manipulation.

Think about this in a military war, two seemingly unrelated forces are trying to destroy the opposer. Having no true connections to their personal history or purpose, they are desperately trying to end the life or advancement of the other.

What can cause such a hatred or emotion so strong as to take the life of another; fear on both ends are the only causation. So in fact, the unseeingly relation between the two is fear indeed.

Ask yourself, who stands to benefit from the horrid consequences of fear based actions.

Who manipulates the mind to otherwise fuel the flames of certain destruction. Such a force isn't your ex, your co-worker nor another of a different race or culture.

This enemy, is the real enemy and he only has the power of influence over an insecure mind. Feeding mercilessly on people's guilt, fears and vices.

Guard your mind from this attack, it takes practice but it can be done. Remember, the first step to overcoming this evil involves forgiveness of self; that is through the humble repentance to God from a sinful lifestyle.

Take this journey for it is your destiny! Take what has been given and nourish its greatness, because ultimately this is what's needed for you to take that first key step; claim it!

Deuteronomy 5:33

"Ye shall walk in all the ways which the LORD your God hath commanded you, that ye may live, and that it may be well with you, and that ye may prolong your days in the land which ye shall possess."

- King James Bible

3 CHAPTER

FOCUS YOUR POWER

Not all walk "the path" at the same pace, just be aware in which your chosen direction takes you. Even leaders were once humble followers, reminding us "we are one." What remains is the manifestation of self-induced fear within your consciousness.

Judging is wasteful, acknowledgement is useful. So until enlightenment is reached, stand deeply rooted in the nourishment of your soil. Until your fear is conquered, judge no one and uproot from stillness and bask in the acknowledgment of your created purpose.

The path in which I speak is best described as, the seeker of truth, a devoted follower or finding mindfulness in christ. Whether it's in relationship, education or even today's politics; seek this truth.

The point is, don't get distracted from your God given purpose! Now is the time to remain focused on your goals, focused on your visualized destination and above all as mentioned, focused on your mindfulness in christ.

As written in my previous book THE CONSCIOUS-NESS OF MAN, I revealed the purposeful explanation behind such a title, it goes as follows.

"The consciousness of man depicts the complete awareness of self, mind, body and soul. It speaks upon all of mankind as a unity, equaling the sum total of our spiritual convictions."

Let's break this down a bit, being it applies to the unfolding wisdom gained throughout your life's overall journey.

When I speak of consciousness and the depiction, I'm trying to relate the awareness of our actions or result thereof. This means learning from not only our own personal mishaps but also the mistakes of others worldwide.

We have in this era an almost infinite amount of information and resources to learn from, so truthfully if humanity was an overall importance to us, we'd take the time to learn, care and commit to the continuation of peace on earth; regardless of race, creed or color.

This is what I mean by "the sum total of our spiritual convictions." I care, you care but how do we choose to express our care? How do we reach out and care for the ones who need care, especially if we're struggling for care ourselves.

This is where the unfathomable wisdom of the Holy Spirit steps in but first we must rid ourselves from all atrocities, burdens or gilts.

You can't help others on the path, if your baggage is weighing you down.

Imagine a barrel of water strapped to your back as you bend to pull someone from drowning, inadvertently you'd hinder their gasp for much needed air. This is where the "complete awareness of self, mind, body and soul" has great significance.

In other words after you've gained knowledge from the path well traveled you'd be qualified, anointed and well equipped to help lead by example; a well known trait of whom is endowed with wisdom of the spirit. This is where the power embedded in you will arise.

When you think you can't handle any more burden, God applies more because he knows what you're truly made of. This is because when the time comes, you'll be able to handle the weight of others burden with ease; including your children's, spouses or friends.

In this upon finding ourselves awakened to the natural order of God's intention, can we realize and hold ourselves accountable for either the negative or positive consequences resulting from our actions.

The afterwards of these actions hold great power, only now can the spoken ideas, intentions or professed forethought can be acknowledge by the truth of its result!

Results are refutable, results are the evidence of one's actions and from this, the absolute in truth is revealed. Let no one's spoken character or professed purpose sway you from the result of his or her actions.

This is one of the simplest forms of wisdom, best understood by accepting truth, do this swiftly soon after witnessing through your experience. Seems obvious but ask yourself, how many times have you suffered the negative consequences of a personal routine or behavior displayed by either yourself or someone close to you?

In other words, if the rhetorical behavior or personal choice yields the same negative results, one would be guilty of having lack of wisdom. Simply put, it is unwise to sit idly by and allow wickedness to manifest if one's knowledge of the outcome is already known.

Upon this path of seeking wisdom, you must first adhere to the natural law of the obvious. This applies to all that would otherwise lead you astray, but by way of empathy, you'd follow them anyway.

Apprehensively or not, you are embedded with powerful intuition so you must become aware of the obviousness of one's own self denial.

Remember in what you seek, steady your perception and listen closely to your heart. If done in all honesty, you will remain steadfast and not fall to the deceit of false prophets and bewildered minds.

Please become more aware that people will openly speak of their heartfelt intentions or promises! They'll express their greatest beliefs or futuristic ideas to convince you of their own personal visions but remember "to each their own!"

Especially when you're on the righteous path of becoming whom you were created to be; please follow your calling.

Again this is why focus, focus, focus is so important at this stage in your journey. Upon this walk people of negative and positive spirits will be drawn to you're glowing light of inspiration.

So how do you decipher the good from the bad? Listen, breathe and steady your present direction forward. If someone comes along besides you and slows your progress in any circumstance or way, consider it a good indication, they may not be spiritually conducive to your purpose. In this, faithfully speak peace along your stride and keep moving forward!

If one comes along and confirms your walk by keeping the pace, soulful understanding or spiritual support, use this opportunity to uplift each other; more so when trials suddenly arise!

A positive person will see you through the tough times, whereas a negative person will only see, enhance and bring light to your troubles. Complaining about trials and tribulations only slows the process of your intended lesson.

Don't just see the issue, trial or problem, see through the issue, absorb and learn from all angles of the circumstances.

This will not only strengthen and prevent you from making similar mistakes but more importantly, help others from making the same.

Such is wisdom, birthed from the experience of a well worn path, traveled faithfully by your calling.

There is no other way to receive but by the willingness to follow the path created for you; life is so much better when you find your purpose, passion and peace. This is why the following of the word of God is so detrimentally important.

Some would seek to gain wisdom by other means; be warned. Only corrupted knowledge is gained, when one seeks only what is comfortable to his soul.

There inlays the problem, most seek the comfortability and desires of the soul. Only remember the makeup of the soul is the go-between the spirit and the temple created as your physical image.

In other words, the composition of the soul is the acquired makeup of one's personal experiences, learn morals and emotion over the course of their lives. Who's to say these experiences were pleasant fill or to a greater degree, knowledge filled.

This would lead to the acknowledgement, that not everyone has the same emotional content, goals or perspectives on life, reasoning or purpose.

This is why I stated "not all walk the path at the same pace." Some witness harder, some speak wiser and some simply try more diligently to figure things out.

So it goes to say the content of the soul, determines the push of one's true purpose, if accepted as their life goal. Which again, is why we must fill our temple with the content and safeguards of wisdom.

So why the struggle, why the fight to gain what has already been given since birth? The reason is far more simplistic than most want to accept, being many have lost their way in the world; desperately chasing ideas and dreams that are not their own.

This is why suffering serves great purpose; that is if it's not created intentionally! Suffering creates a discomfort that seemingly slows the concept of time.

Upon reflecting, one should seek a power much greater than their own, a faith that beckons one to fall to their knees and submit to a higher form of understanding. In this, one comes to the understanding that peace is desired.

Bringing forth a freedom from the pain and ultimately the wisdom to become unaffected by the ailments that created the suffering.

The time of hardships will come and pass like the seasons of change, so absorbing the experience can only help you to become stronger. Anything else would be in denial of one's true purpose, again this is where focus comes into play. Push forward, if for no other reason as to not remain stagnant at the minimum of effort.

Remember this is a journey sought after by many but most lose their way; you will not! You have chosen to stay focus for a greater reasoning. You have embarked upon an adventure that was tailored to fit your spiritual likeness.

Enjoy this experience, find the happiness within the presence of your current circumstance. Know that you have the ability to acquire your deepest desires; when truly understood. Make way for unimaginable intellect, as well as a wonderful assortment of things once known but forgotten over time.

In this book, I will show you how to peace the mind and to hear what's being whispered constantly in the spirit. All you have to do is trust, breathe deeply and calm your soul. Allow the presence of the lord to fill your mind upon evacuation of the baggage gained over your lifespan.

You can do this, it has been done and will continue to be done by others who truly seek to find the untapped wisdom within the consciousness of our spirit.

Others of great achievement have acquired this, why not you! You've taken the first necessary steps, now continue to push on. So focus, focus and continue to focus on with all your might!

Luke 10:19

Behold, I give unto you to tread on serpents and scorpions, and over all the power of the enemy: and nothing shall by any means hurt you. - King James Bible

4 CHAPTER

YOUR JOURNEY YOUR LEGACY

You've taken the necessary steps, now prepare for the battle! No worries, you are well equipped with the backing of a phenomenal power; waiting to uphold your purpose throughout this journey. This power is the whisper that will speak to you when you fall, reminding you of why you should get up and continue on.

Furthermore, passing along what is needed to uphold the continuation of purpose, culture and generational knowledge.

Another way of saying this is a wisdom will be shared unto you, by way of the result of your physical and spiritual suffering. With the experience shared well after the knowledge gain and understood, one could now utilize the meekness of wisdom to navigate through the journey of life. Use this to choose your destiny and yes, there are many blessed destinations waiting for you.

Here's a story given to me upon my travels throughout the spirit realm.

One night deep in rest, I was shown by the Holy Spirit over timeless generations, an awareness reminding me to pass on what is true for the continuation of peace and to never forget. Take a moment to really think about this next story.

Remember, this is only the first of many steps and this one in particularly requires you to be completely unselfish, in regard to your opinions.

Being opinions are mostly influenced by others of different reasonings and or purposes, one must boldly stand guard at the gate of their mind, continuously and vigorously; please enjoy.

While on the battlefield of life, if a warrior passed down a sword to his child and the child one day passes down the sword through his family, grandchildren and so forth, does this ever change the battles within and around their lives?

Or does it perpetuate a cycle of learned behaviors towards a traditional association to unresolved problems.

What of the traditions of the presumed enemies, does their families of created warriors share the same traditions of fear and war passed down by the acceptance of the sword? Often we get distracted from the truth in such a way we speak out boldly on ideologies, myths and fears we truly don't understand.

This is why I focus not on the many distractions within our society but rather the purpose God created me to fulfill. In other words finding the mindfulness to otherwise be a benefit to those who'd trust in my focused leadership; furthermore passing safely through the battles plundering through this world.

Know that battles are mostly battles to separate the weak from the war; even more so within the battles of the mind.

Ancient knowledge would also reveal, the concept of horrid possibility during a time of strategic manipulation. Such as ones who engage in an actual physical war may not be the warriors themselves!

Maybe these battles were created to rid the sheep as the wolves claim the land. Even though the remains of the war would undoubtedly reveal that not all wolves rank in knowledge or strength , so in a manner of time they to would war against each other until only the truly selfish remain; starting the cycle over and over again.

This form of lunacy and insecure manifestations would continue, until there is nothing of true value or purpose left in the life span we were created for, hence the true deceptive intentions; behind the wickedness of the wolves.

No different from a game of chess, where the king has authority over this land and the queen displays truth in power.

In the acknowledgment of this analogy, the pawns and chosen subjects are prepared to willingly sacrifice their spoken purposes passed down traditionally as a way of life.

All to fulfill the suggested battles whispered in the ear of a king; majestically cloaked in sheep's wool. My question is, what piece or part do you play in life?

What battles, distractions or opinionated traditions were handed down to you in the form of a sword?

Know that until mindfulness is reached, the principalities of this world will effectively blind you from seeking the truth within your God given purpose.

When this truth is awakened within the embedment of your spirit, you'll be distracted no more.

In this your leadership will prevail as you walk a new path, a path of fulfilled purpose and ultimately a path of peace and wisdom— readily available to pass down; replacing the sword. Journey well my friend and create a legacy worth living over and over again.

With this said, here's a little more clarity on the analogy of the sword passed down from generation to generation. This sword, this idea or symbol can be used for either protection or destruction.

This depends on the perception of security or lack thereof, manifesting in the mindset of the child, student and yes, even the innocence of the bystanders looking up to leadership.

Here's what I'm leading to, if ideas, opinions or traditions are passed down in the ignorance of one's own clouded perceptions, then it would be almost a guarantee the tradition, in whatever capacity will be upheld with fierce dignity, in belief that what was learned is true.

Now get what I'm saying? Can you imagine a world where people could simply wipe the slate clean and start off teaching the youth of the world wisdom, as opposed to what is thought to be true unbiased knowledge. From what I've come to understand, knowledge can be easily influenced by fear, as well as hate and anger.

Which is why the teachers or examples in leadership must be of true mental clarity.

Again, let's break this down a bit deeper, let's tackle the ever present issue of racism; tough subject right? Everyone has their own opinion based off at least three-forms of influences throughout their life.

Its imperative that we're honest with ourselves on such a matter, especially since racism can be easily confused with prejudice or bigotry. Now as far as the "three influences," of what I believe is the makeup of our opinions are as follows and I know there's more but the top three are as follows; cultural upbringings, personal experiences and media.

These three are very powerful influencers regarding your opinions, especially on subjects which most considered to be up-close and personal to their heart or should I say, what some people believe to be the emotions streaming from their heart.

Unfortunately most often than not, people are actually confuse when it comes to the so-called feelings of the heart.

Often when this confusion arises, what's actually taking place is the misconception or the false perceptions allowed to develop in their heads i.e. the clutter of the mind.

In this people often base key information, stereotyping and judgement with confusion and bitter ill will, all in conjunction with the fact that they are simply unfamiliar to their own bias reasoning.

How dangerous is a mind that is so cluttered with confusion that judgement passed down is thought to be just? Their inlays the problem of racism, bigotry, prejudice, hatred and countless other forms of wickedness.

Everyone wants to know how to stop racism or at least most people. The question remains, is the answer actually obtainable when it appears that almost everyone, has their own so called informed "opinions?"

I'm talking actual fear based conceptions, ideas or worse yet, the embedment of evil perceptions; taught by the vileness mindset of a person's insecurities or hate thereof.

Ok let's be honest, we all have some form of prejudice, rarely spoken but practiced almost on every occasion. Oh you're not prejudice, not even a little bias on a particular subject? Ok, so who's your pick Ohio State football or Michigan?

Do you like anchovies or pineapple on your pizza, Why? Did you vote for a man to become president because you'd come to the conclusion, that you couldn't trust the opposing female candidate? Or was your vote more cynical, believing that you'd actually get a higher tax break because of your skin color?

Let's face it, some people vote like they're buying expensive clothes. They see a media influenced ad/campaign and quickly come to the conclusion, that appearing like minded will catapult them to a higher form of status. Only issue is, that which truly dwells within one's mind. Truthfully, it's all a mask or image one's trying to project from time to time; such is the journey of finding one's self.

We're all guilty of masks at some point in our lives, reason being we've somehow learned to go with the hetero-suggestive flow. Now remember, life's a process and if done well we live, we learn and we grow; just be aware of what you're growing into.

Now being completely candid, most people have no real idea of who the presidential candidates really are.

The masses don't know them on a personally level, not even close to being buddies or old acquaintances and they certainly don't have the ability or personal connection to call a candidate up for a dinner invite.

Yet most create a savage political divide on their jobs, between friendships and even their homes; fiercely defending they're so-called political status. Why?

Because of the perpetual bombardment of distractions, pulling us helplessly towards other forms of unhealthy attention-getters.

In this, we have no idea of where we're headed! All this based off the actuality, that someone persuaded them to vote on a position, perceived to best suit their personal insecurities or interests.

Now touching back on the issues regarding prejudice and the like thereof. Considering the vastness of the subject, here's a quick sum up; repent, rethink and renew your mind within the next paragraph.

The stereotypes of prejudices bigotry or racism culti-vated by society are nothing more than the embedment of opinionated cultural norms, often insidiously nurtured from childhood.

The good news is we can grow, learn and evaluate as adults, then make informed decisions or personal choices. This in turn can break the constricting chain of mental slavery, camouflaged within miseducation and insecurities. Free the thoughts that are not your own and arise into en-lightenment. Your view of life and how it operates are much better from this heightened perception of thought.

Remember to be subjective to eternal wisdom while walking this path; anything else may grossly influence your opinions in a negative fashion.

Opinions, opinions, and even more opinions, often proudly stood up for by misinformed influences for per-sonal gain.

Again, often these "so-called opinions" are merely ideas passed down from culture to culture, but will there ever come a time when the vast majority says enough is enough, in regard to the hatred of another human being?

So to sum it all up, to seek wisdom amongst other forms of peace, one must accept the responsibility to chance, challenge and change the thought processes of the world.

Mind dump the sweet ignorance of opinionated biases and the flow of timeless wisdom will fill in its place. Bottom line, lose the mindset crafted by the world and reset your mind to that of wisdom.

In this you'll be fully prepared for the battle, the multitude of mishaps or any devilish plans set to detour your purpose. Now go, push forward and place yourself amongst the greatest of legacy's; journey well.

Tobit 5:16

"So they were well pleased. Then said he to Tobias, Prepare thyself for the journey, and God send you a good journey. And when his son had prepared all things for the journey, his father said, Go thou with this man, and God, which dwelleth in heaven, prosper your journey and the angel of God keep you company."

-King James Bible

5 CHAPTER

SHAME, SHAME; JUDGE NOT

Often in times of inspiration, a higher sense of self aris-es as a shield of confidence. When this happens, be careful and judge not of others who are frantically going through the motions of life's personal building blocks.

In this be the leader you aspire to become and don't allow yourself to fall back on a time when someone treated you negatively during your trial and era. In other words, don't become "that person."

It's often easy and primarily over looked, when we find ourselves stringently focused and in good position, then unknowingly falling into that mr. or mrs. goody-two-shoes category and being labeled, "That person." In this, it's even easier to become judgmental when others are going through a "not so good" position in life. Ever wonder why?

Why are most so judgmental and desensitized to the pain and misery of others?Why at times does it appear as though many actually get excited, when another person is going through certain personal failures, trying times and or problematic circumstances?

Remember, we've all at some point in time encountered difficulties.

It is at these moments of trial and era, when the process of learning from our mistakes, exponentially grows into what we were created to become.

Inversely, if trial and era is not learned from during your growth process, it will diminish your drive and true potential. This resulting in the reseeding of your purpose, placing you short of achieving your goals and widely missing the mark of your destined legacy.

Take faith in knowing the stressors and fears we've encountered, served as the greater purpose of overcoming the obstacles created in life. In this, the wisdom gained by the circumstances overcame, has become the experience needed to carve in stone.

This knowledge is now utilize as an instrument and a catalyst to help countless others across the world. Please understand, we as mankind should refuse to judge the singularities of one's stumble or corrupted mindset, especially since we've all been through difficulties at times.

One again please remember during times of these difficulties, we are not always a true representation of ourselves but more so, how we respond and deal with the issues; this does in fact reflect our level of spiritual maturity or the lack thereof.

If fear or insecurities are manifesting within the temple of a person's trials, it's easy to believe they are enemies to someone who's not currently struggling. This is why we should flee from the judging and labeling of others.

Instead listen, learn from, love and pray for the day we share 'as one" in the purpose of our heavenly father's intentions.

In this it's possible to forgive the bigotry, anger and hatred displayed in society, even the turned backs, the unbelievers and naysayers as well can be pardoned while struggling through their confused times.

Let's be honest, what's that little voice in the back of our minds, when we first get bad news about that,"one particular" person at work.

You know, that one coworker who finally gets caught in a lie and embarrassed or worse yet, is suddenly getting divorced or their car gets repossessed at the most inopportune time possible?

I realize this may not necessarily make you a bad or negative person but like most, we may have grown a bit insensitive and as previously mentioned, desensitized to the welfare of others.

Being you're currently on the righteous path of receiving wisdom through experience, be cautious not to become judgmental.

Your focus at this moment should be of empathy and spiritual awareness within the matter, as it does pertain to the current opportunity of helping someone in need.

Know that when a person is going through and you've become aware of it, actually develops into a blessing in disguise for both parties!

Why? Because on one side if you're blessed with good standing, it allows for the opportunity of more spiritual growth.

On the other side, the person going through witnesses the power of love, compassion and empathy at their most insecure and transparent moment in life. In this they can see first hand, you as a leadership model, leading by example as the body of christ and reaching out in support of helping them through their trials.

It happens first by ignoring that, "Holier than thou"mentality that sneaks up behind you saying," I just knew it!" or "Hey everyone, did you hear about such and so? Well, I heard that he said that she said . . ."

After extinguishing this still small flame from becoming an all-out firestorm, defamation of character or community roast on your fellow mankind. Quickly give thanks for being in the privileged position in which you have the strength and mental clarity to be of help.

Not to forget, if you've survived what the person in need is stumbling through, it's a spiritual duty to give a helping hand. This helping hand is now more prevalent than ever if you've been helped yourself or know of resources of professionalism, friends or ministries of help.

Also if you've journeyed the path of my stubbornness, you are endowed even more so if the path you took, involved invoking the pure will of commitment, catapulting you into a higher understanding!

Know that these issues in life are what I call spiritual character building moments, and they are no different from the cleaning agent added to a washing machine.

Remember, the detergent you add to your washing machine is considered harsh to that of dirt and grime, this serves as a pretty good analogy as to how things or circumstances are added in our everyday lives; furthermore helping us to target problematic issues by cleaning them up.

That is, the struggles we face in life are meant to be harsh at times but by the end of the cycle you'll be fresh to take on another day.

Resisting the cycles or temperatures within the trials and tribulations as it turns, tumbles and rinses the dirt and miseries away, will only add more debris, i.e. unresolved issues weighing and slowing your life process down.

Ultimately the evading of cleansing cycles set within your life, will soon clog up and stop your forward progress; resulting in loss of your true potential.

Shame, shame if you take the opportunity to seize another person's "spiritual character building" moment to judge, ridicule or gossip. Wasn't there a time when you inadvertently created a bad circumstance for yourself? Maybe made a foolish decision? Unjustly ridiculed the wrong person?

Come on, remember when you were coerced into believing, "He or she wouldn't tell" or "it's our little secret" and somehow your so-called private business gets out anyway?

Believe it or not, don't fault the false friend who told; fault the weakness within you that committed the act!

Take full responsibility of the consequences, learn from them and redeem yourself by the corrective actions of solving problems created. To do this, first start by asking for forgiveness; then share your feelings.

With the openness of your heartfelt mistake and with the honest intention on never choosing that particular path again; move on.

Yes, move on and do so without fail! Lift yourself from the vice-like grip manifestation of guilt and continue to push forward.

How we live our lives creates the very essence of mistakes, some in sequence, one right after another; that is until we learn, accept and resolve with God.

No time to waste, course correct with a new purpose , remembering that people are watching, people are talking and most of all; people are in need of you to be a leader.

This is why we seek, why we thrive and rise to achieve eternal knowledge. With this meek understanding, let humbleness be your guide, never forget your place and even more so; your created purpose.

Maybe there was simply a time when you made a difficult choice trying to fit in and you were inadvertently taken through years of struggle, say after trying drugs, alcohol, what about the residual effects of sexual or mental abuse.

We often deem ourselves worthy but honestly we can't truly understand how fragile the human mind, body and soul can be; nor do we know just how strong it can become.

Do note the next time you or someone passes by a vagrant, the homeless or the like thereof, take a mental moment and focus your spiritual vibration on love for this person.

Instead of judging the character in bondage, acknowledge their struggle to survive.

Maybe it was post traumatic stress fighting for your freedom or beaten and incarcerated for years standing up for a just cause, Maybe they were born into a family of predators, who knows.

Here's a few things you can quickly acknowledge while passing by, they didn't give up on life and jump off a building, landing on your new car.

Rarely can I imagine this person pulling out a weapon to assault or rob you, neither can I envision this person seeking to verbally tear your spirit down in judgement for mistakes that you've made in the past.

I realize we're in a judgmental world of Dr. Phil recordings, redundant reality television shows about housewives and man made hustlers of business or street wealth. Also, not to forget the overly sensationalistic soap operas, acronymic detective shows and created Hollywood dramas of who's dating who and what's in and out of fashion.

Understand the big setup is to dilute our natural conscious way of thinking, to that of believing we are better than everyone else!

Imagine a city where everyone had it crammed into their minds, that all other cities around them were deemed inferior, less than or beneath their perceived way of life.

Absolutely nothing positive would develop of such thinking! It would only result in challenge and competition. Everyone living in fear, trying to outwork their neighbors, become more intelligent and clever than their neighbors and at all cost, at the minimum, emerge physically stronger than those who'd be considered our neighbors.

This fear, this insatiable drive that one must push to become the hierarchy at all cost, is birth from wickedness.

What makes us strong as a human species is our ability to come together and intertwine. When this comes to pass, we've created a bond of physical and mental strength readily available to withstand any trials set out to divide our species.

This is how we emerge as a new consciousness in christ, coming together, learning, loving and helping each other. This is the only way wisdom can once again become a natural part of our existence on earth.

Imagine passing down and learning from truthful knowledge shared within the spirit. Blessed experiences, parables, analogies and examples all shared with peace to advance our future purposes.

Without this accomplishment, what's left when mental barriers are suddenly faced with physical limitations, insecurities and fears?

It most assuredly boil down to anarchy, that is who's believed to be the so-called hierarchy and or physically strongest readily preparing for battle, which is often the type who's willing to kill for insecurities sake.

Isn't this what mentally happens when we choose to believe we're better or superior over the weak and needy? You wanna know what true strength is? Talk to a woman that's been raped or had an abortion and chose to pull her life together regardless of people's opinion or pain.

Try asking an alcoholic or heroin addict what is was like going through withdrawals and struggling to recover their job, family and self respect.

What of a soldier fighting on foreign soil, only to encounter their presumed enemy is actually fighting for their own land, freedom and families right to life.

What of a person who's dealt with a sudden loss, in either finance, family or health, yet chooses not to turn their back on society and God's overall purpose.

Here's a quick thought, the next time a person of interest less fortunate than most starts to plead, lie or does"whatever"to manipulate you while in they're struggling state, ask yourself if you could do better in their position?

Most often, the average person cringes at the thought of resisting a sugary treat, a cigarette break or a deep rich cup of coffee, even though they know its not what the doctor prescribed; let alone trying to overcome depression or any other mental disease, health wise or spiritual matter.

Honestly, would you be a better human being in the circumstance of temporary mental capacity loss? Would you choose to beg, borrow or steal as opposed to committing murder for your next fix, hunger pain or greed?

Here's what I've come to learn as I became enlightened, Judge not because not everyone is strong enough to handle certain burdens in life.

Maybe, just maybe God created them to be that much more stronger, being they actually have the strength to overcome the adversity! And in doing so keep you focused and humble while presenting the opportunity for you to be a blessing yourself.

Know that when I say being a blessing, I'm talking about the affordability of real, physical sacrifice. I'm not just talking about praying and hoping someone would "get better," but actually becoming hands-on as to physically find a safe way to inspire.

If they have a flat tire for instance use your AAA, if they are down and out and need money for clothes to find work, ask them their clothes or shoe size!

Don't just hand them a bible, don't just quote a scripture from memory so fast even a typographer couldn't record it but rather get hands on their circumstance and lead by example; this can be done either close or afar.

Please don't fall into that, "Waste of time" gossiping about their unfortunate issues, after all maybe you're not afflicted because you lack the strength to overcome?

Point is we don't really know who we are or who we'll become in the midst of the struggle. That is until darkness has fallen, and suddenly we find ourselves stuck between a rock and a hard place, as the water level within this bind starts to rise around us.

Want to know what's a real shame? Having the complete use of your mind, bodily functions, resources financially and spiritually, yet choosing to completely ignore, gossip about or point the finger at another human being for their personal stumbling blocks, financial circumstances, or failures.

Shame if all your physical and mental capacities are in order to optimum functionality but you choose to look down on others struggling, on top of do nothing of true value with your life!

Know that the tipping scale of life can at any given time shift against you, leaving you in a bind and testing your strength; who's to say you'd do better than the next.

Are you strong enough to handle adultery? Brave enough to sacrifice your years on the job and financial security for just cause? Can you handle the pain from a serious accident without becoming dependent on drugs meant to ease that pain or peace of mind? Know that most people live on a week to week basis and some strictly monthly basis.

Again, at any given time what if the unthinkable happened and you suffer a loss or serious financial hit; leaving you without any resources in your physical or spiritual account?

This is where awareness of self becomes essential, if you've invested positive time in others you may have a foundation readily available to help.

If you've studied and research bible based scriptures, parables and practiced the teaching in your everyday lives, you'll have the ability to lean on the word of God at crisis times in your life.

No one grows up saying, "I want to fall into depression, become a prostitute (this includes on the street, in a relationship or within the work environment!), drug addict or alcoholic, just to name a few, being that life or how we choose to live it affects people on so many levels.

Seriously, can you imagine what it's actually like to be that person going through?

Or do you simply, yet inadvertently deviate to being "that one person" of sound mind and body, judging another for their misguided choices or non-choice of lifestyle?

Please, if we're to rise our state of mind to that of true christ consciousness, which is the state of mindfulness Christ taught for our peace and salvation; we must turn from our judgmental ways.

If to become a society of true clarity or even the likeness of enlightenment, please for the sake of his mercy bestowed unto this world, don't become the type of person that chooses to point out other people's flaws or circumstances.

At times of this nature, its detrimental for our growth in wisdom to show empathy and leadership; in this readily available to help if called upon.

In reference to the title "Shame, Shame; Judge not." Know that the people going through the struggle didn't choose this particular way of life. So in reference to a person's choice of "being," reflecting on a judgmental attitude, should shy away from ridicule, whether directly or indirectly towards the person in need.

Just remember, we are at times on different levels of achievements and time frames, so how a person functions and deals with their problems, may not be as swift as others would want or think.

Yet recall, it's not about the opinions of others pertaining to someone else's personal growth but rather, the mindfulness in Christ, ushering in the wisdom needed while going through the affliction of their personal journey.

Furthermore, this could also include the people "of struggle,"as the functional alcoholic, the misguided other woman or man, falling into the denial of actually believing the adulterer is getting a divorce.

Point is, even if you're the one going through; don't become judgmental to others! Maybe the mindset of a person spiritually dying, whether in a difficult relationship, trial of financial instability or current security issues, are actually meant to go through this season of their lives!

This in part as their consequence for learning never to go down that path again!

Hence why if you position yourself to help, judgement is not the key but rather your applied knowledge gained in Christ.

In this, the wisdom of your spiritual journey acquired, can help guide the needy to the word of God and how it applies to their lives.

Also remember, the currently "down and out" doesn't have to look the part, again just make sure you're NOT the one judging; because this is a win-win for the demonically influenced.

Remember this is a transformational time for those who've taken the stand of assisting those who seek enlightenment. That is the stand of diligent purpose, pushing them towards the path of their God given abilities to achieve abundance on earth as in heaven.

Again, this starts by clearing your mind of the embedment of clutter, affording you the time to understand who you are in the mindfulness of Christ.

This as opposed to the mindset obtained by the principalities and strongholds of the world; which in fact are not pertinent to your personal development. Remembering to focus and spiritually meditate on who you are in christ, instead of trying to solve the issues of others ill prepared.

This will expedite your journey towards your abundant destiny. In this the natural order of sought after wisdom, will effortlessly yield the ability to help others in the wholeness of your completion.

It's never as easy as we'd like it to be but God's favor, mercy and love will be with you always as to encourage you throughout this process.

Not to forget, the multitude in need are always watching, waiting and praying for tangible much needed help.

Prepare yourself, you have been blessed with amazing abilities; please utilize your faith and use your gifts wisely.

Romans 2:19

"And art confident that thou thyself art a guide of the blind, a light of them which are in darkness,"

- King James Bible

6 CHAPTER

THE LIKENESS OF LOVE

While on this journey, let's take a moment to reflect on a time much simpler within the youthfulness of our memories. A not so long ago time, when time itself seemingly had no real barren, purpose or meaning; that is unless we desperately wanted something.

In fact the seconds lost through the day, unknowingly taken for granted by childhood ambitions only slowed when our desires became a focus point for our wants, spoils or needs. Times such as these inspired relentless energy and enthusiasm, better described as impatience by our parents.

Only what was thought to be impatience, was merely our youth dealing with what appeared to be an eternity when in need of what we desired at that very moment. Can you remember a time such as this?

That youthful jittery wit, the notion you couldn't sit still because the "ants-in-your pants that'll make you dance" phenomenon can so on?

Can you remember spinning in circles with your arms stretched afar until dizziness became that of uncontrollable laughter?

These were the timeless moments so very important as the building blocks of our lives but again, enter wants and desires and suddenly time slows to that of eternity.

Now at some point the mindset starts to change from small ideas to big ones, then on to our perceptions and how we're view and accepted by others.

Interestingly this often comes up around the same time erupting hormones meticulously presents itself. Then almost instantaneously and without thought, we simply can't wait to grow up; hence the feeling of eternity!

Remember this pattern by keeping in touch with the innocence of your youth, it's a good key in realizing how changes in acceptance can unknowingly occur. Changes such as seeking out the likeness of love, when in fact it's not love at all but a watered down version of what we've come to believe is the act of someone loving us.

More specifically, this sheds light on the love of our parents embraced us with as children, on one hand there's the love within being a responsible parent and on the other, there's the hugs, tickles to the belly and kisses to a scraped knee.

This kindness and warm embedded certain memories, needs and desires that we'll seek for the rest of our lives but this comes with caution.

What of a child who's gone through the difficulties of a broken home or abuse? What happens to the mindset of the innocent when the hardships of life are shared within the ranks of the family? In this case from young to old, a child often bares the burdens of life much too early, furthermore bringing an unbalanced mindset to fruition.

Here lies the often unknowingly, yet much sought after "likeness of love," in other words whatever makes them feel accepted, appreciated or liked.

In a time when brokenness seemingly becomes a person's reality, society shuns or labels this person of struggle as different, strange or simply not in touch. This cause and effect over one's social hardships in turn, makes them feel isolated and eventually different from most others.

The latter of this is, people of brokenness starts to subconsciously seek out acceptance from whomever or whatever mimics the likeness of the love we all desire.

Eventually this leads to a person saying "I'm fine with who I am," or "I love me for me" and lastly, "This is who I am, accept me for me!" Know that loving yourself is a good thing but finding who you really are is most important, before loving what you believe your physical or mental outcome has lead you to believe.

Another way of looking at this is, the world wants you to look, act and feel a certain way in which to be labeled as a group.

Upon falling for the principalities and strongholds ideas of who you are and what group you prescribe to, you can now be lead, manipulated and persuaded to do the will of the wicked.

How did we get to this point? We were just at loving ourselves and seeking out love right? Don't be fooled by the crafty ways of the opposer!

Remember I said keep "in touch with the innocence of your youth, it's a good key in realizing how changes in acceptance can unknowingly occur." The key is to avoid falling for swift acceptance, in place of what has already been given by God!

Remember a desperate person seeks the swiftness of attention, this often comes with a terrible price. In this, the desperate act falls for less than what is deserved and soon a paradigm is established; lowering one's goals, ambitions and projective outlook for their lives.

Again, the key is realizing not to lose our focus on love but to actively seek it out. Not by way of looking for the likeness of one's desires and acceptance but the actual calling embedded in our hearts, in other words; seek God for the fulfilling of love in your life!

You can't blame your parents, your upbringings or the people around you, it's easy to do but forgive the distractions of others so you can get back to really loving who you were created to be and again that's not what the world wants!

The world wants you to fit in a group but also there's a twist of manipulation lurking, have you noticed the rebellious images in the media over the last few years? Standing up and announcing "it's okay to be you," "do your own thing," and eventually "You are the universe!"

Building one's self esteem is important but when you start believing in yourself more than the God who created you, things start to get a bit shady.

Trust when I say confusion develops when we start making idols out ourselves.

In this the mental act of separatism seeks in, convincing us that we are not only different but we are our own masters of life; ultimately willing the powers of the universe to do our bidding.

Soon with God almost forgotten as our go-to for healing, direction and love, we scamper down the much easier path of finding ourselves through meditation, sought after enlightenment of that of seeking mindfulness.

Again, this is what the world is offering as the acceptance much sought after in place of the love of God. Mentally ask yourself and be totally honest, do you trust your spouse, friend or boss unconditionally, 100% without a doubt through any hardships, trials or circumstance in life?

Here's an even better question, do you trust yourself, unconditionally, 100% without a doubt through any hardships, trials or circumstance in life?

Please be completely honest with yourself, being at times we are so quick to say "yes, I know myself and I trust in the decisions I've made!"

Only the question isn't about your decisions, it's solely "do you really trust yourself?" If believed so then answer this question "has your spouse, friend or boss ever told you a lie? Even better, have you ever lied to yourself?

Take for instance, failure to stop smoking, drinking, gossiping or even overeating to lose weight.

If you're like the mass majority of people myself included, you're not perfect and we all at sometimes have fallen short of our blessed potential.

So in reference to the world influencing us to meditate, reach enlightenment or find mindfulness within our not-so-perfect selves, be warned and bring light to what we're really manifesting, which is to the fullest extent; our sinful nature.

Know that when we turn from God to seek healing, peace and abundance within the clutter of our minds, we only manifest lies, denials and insecurities. Please know that the wickedness in this world has stretched out to those who don't bury their sins in alcohol, drugs, sex or violence.

Now it stretches to devour and manipulate the spiritually and physically strong; whispering money, power and respect above others.

Seeking out those who didn't break, those that has surpassed and have conquered the smaller battles in life and now are on to influence the world in a positive way.

Finding God as the answer to love and not the settlement of childish needs and desires seeking attention.

Speaking of childhood, let's get back to that innocent time when life was a bit more carefree and without worry. Traveling back to remembering when the word 'like' was in our minds, more exciting than the word love.

Here's a little story that helps me remember through times of stress and everyday worry that my life is just a part of life, so I might as well contribute with my bests efforts.

Like most stories it starts with a simple question of heart; do you remember passing along that handwritten note, where you actually drew, on paper the check boxes awaiting a mark "do you like me, yes or no?

How this applies to wisdom is just as important with any question, that is questions that are seriously asked for the purposes of much needed feedback.

Ok this requires a slow down, so again let's ease into the nostalgic memories of our childhood, it's not like its light speed or even close but things change over the course of time, so enjoy this brief look into the past.

What's nice about slowing down is the reminiscing of the innocence of that childlike question, summoning nervous breath of fresh air soon buried away by the sands of time.

Recalling these moments are far from the whimsical recollections camouflaged as day dreaming, being they still reside fresh in your heart-field; reuniting a love of life at times so easily forgotten.

Just know that at any given moment in your life, the power of heart can be called upon desire. This calling will usher in a transformation more powerful than any figure conjured by imagination; this can bring about a tangible reality if diligently sought after!

Finding a way to reach this place in your mind, will assist when needed the most upon finding your enlighten path, but first one must forget, leave behind and forsake the wastefulness of cluttered baggage.

Upon completion of this burden a resurrection of freedom once blissfully enjoyed will come rushing back into your life.

Getting back to the note, can you remember the nostalgic thoughts of nervousness yet inquisitive feelings rumbling in your belly, all the while by sitting in the same class as your schoolmate love?

Can you recall the chill of goosebumps arising, as you anxiously awaited an answer from that crush, just two desks down?

How jittery your fingers were when you forced the words onto paper, before passing it along with hopes of getting a glimpse of a received smile?

Whatever happen to those days of simpler thought with just a hint of mischief in curiosity? Remember flying a kite or holding hands while taking a long walk?

What about going to the park where there's already a BBQ grill built in?

Remember when a few dollars made you feel wealthy beyond your wildest dreams, because it was all yours to spend at the candy store? Have we lost this simpler way of life by way of age, time or regret?

Red light-Green light anyone? How about freeze tag or possibly playing jacks?

No different from your tree climbing, skateboarding pavement scraped knee, these light hearted fun filled days are still apart of who you are, still deeply embedded within your mental storehouse.

Only after years of the cultural melting pot, SAT scores, bills and overstimulation of news report and reality shows, just to name a few.

The mind has been overwhelmed with unnecessary stress filled issues, financial instabilities, relationship insecurities and self-inflicted guilt stimulated paranoia.

Also not to forget, the ever growing battle within our own exhausted state of consciousness, trying to live up to standards created by entities of purpose-filled deception.

The gravity of such problematic concerns inadvertently over time, tends to weigh down and suppress those bliss filled, carefree days. This is what I referred to as, "One must first forget."

Remember feeling protected and accepted? No worries whatsoever, because you knew someone was there when you needed to be picked up, held or rocked to sleep? Just how do we rekindle those nostalgic days of joy?

The answer is much easier than most are ready to accept, even though we've been hearing it sporadically through our lives!

Remember you have the power to change your reality by changing the way you perceive your environment to be, as mentioned this breath of life still resides in you; so let's take a peak.

Again, recall from the innocence from your mind, as you stuck your hand out the car window, while your parents drove the scenic route to take in the sunset.

As the chill of the wind flowed through your fingers, up and down as you glided through the air, what was on your mind? Absolutely nothing, at least nothing when it came to the previous stressors mentioned.

It was simply the unawareness of stressors, you were free to imagine and unknowingly take for granted that all was right in the world, why? Because you felt safe.

You were protected to feel free and now, somehow we've all grown up feeling the weight of the world subsequently surpassing that feeling of peace. So how do we "not think?"

How do we become thoughtless of unnecessary responsibilities, fears and false representations leading to a since of low self worth?

One way is to again, remember and avoid that childhood pattern which allowed us to fall for the perception of the likeliness of love.

Another way, instead of struggling to rekindle the past, focus more on the word of God. For me and countless others, it gave us the ability to say we now are free to enjoy the present and all its abundance, joy and happiness.

With a mind less weighted down by the clutter of confusions, misconceptions and miseducation, I as well as yourselves can walk into the future, enlightened with the total peace of acquiring wisdom along the journey.

Mark 12:31

"And the second is like, namely this, Thou shalt love thy neighbor as thyself. There is none other commandment greater than these." - King James Version

7 CHAPTER

THE THREE ROUTES

Understanding change is often difficult because it deals with the very core of whom we've grown to become. This is why there's so many self-help books and products scattered within the world. Unfortunately it has become unimaginably profitable so one must wonder in the mindset of supply and demand, is it even worth fixing the issue or should the powers that be, cash in on the products stating "how we can become a better version of yourselves."

This is the mindset of what I've come to call the entrepreneurship of endless wonder, the often unfortunate thing is, it works! Only there's a catch, if you're buying into another's idea, you're actually paying for the image of the supplier not who you were created to be.

In other words you can spend hundreds of thousands of dollars in school to become the professional you desire but is the profession you desire, for financial resource only or for the actual benefit of your time on earth; what of the need of others.

Also it doesn't have to be about money spent, because something vastly more important is often used up as well; I'm speaking of time.

How much time does the average person spend on finding out what their work in life is going to be, how about the love of oneself or that of others, what of the seemingly elusive purpose of one's journey?

No stressors, all will come to those who seek for the glory of God's plans to come to pass.

In time of continuous questions, ever wonder is there a balance of enjoyment in your life or are you a slave to a title or maybe someone else's image of you.

Point is, have you fulfilled the purpose of your creation or has your life's mission been swayed away by the products of endless searches perceived to be that of happiness and abundance.

We all have different levels of strength, so what worked for me upon my spiritual walk of diligence, may not work or appeal to you but even still, maybe you can find what works better in God's grace. Here are the three routes that I took to get on the path of sought after wisdom.

First to seek wisdom is to become enlightened but know there are many levels of enlightenment. On one level I was shown enlightenment by way of dreams and visions, although this was pure bliss, it swiftly came with a high spiritual price or rather a detrimental choice for life in the present; I'll give more detail to how serious this choice was a little later on.

Secondly, which is actually an alternate of the first enlightened path, is first to accept the things within the world we cannot change, but develop faith that all can be done by the grace of God.

If enlightenment isn't your first initial route, try becoming "the protector"yourself, for the rekindling of your spouse's joy, family or friends.

In other words, however you imagine to be loved, taken care of and spoiled; be that for your loved ones.

Humbly love them as unconditionally as you'd like and you'll get a since of the strength it takes to be that protector, that forgiver and ultimately the leader by which you'd want God to be for you.

Are you strong enough for this challenge? The answer is absolutely not! No one is, because God is the almighty, he created us in his own image and loves you more than the likeness of love we've come to accept as human beings.

In this you'll see truth revealed, as to remind you of your own blessed innocence also. This means the total sacrifice of yourself! Furthermore and again, you'd draw out that beautiful childlike peace within your significant other's heart, changing their perception as well!

Upon diligent consistency you'll eventually see the confirmation of miracles and find that its reciprocal between the both of you.

Lastly of the three routes chosen, I put on the armor that is the word of God from the King James version bible. Simply put, I geared up for spiritual cognition; that is you must vigorously do battle within the battlefield of your mind.

In this laying waste to all your lust, vices and manifested guilt trips created over time, but know this isn't truly possible unless you submit to a power much higher than human potential.

The point is to reconnect to that childlike freedom, never questioning yourself based off the wicked idolized perceptions scattered within the world.

Know this, upon christ's sacrifice you are free, but upon the wiles of your own guilt, you are damned. This is why transformation into mindfulness of Christ's teachings enables the wisdom needed for your happiness, as well as others within your environment.

Once this is found, you'll see just how beautiful this world is, as well as the beauty within your purpose.

In my personal journey of enlightenment, I accomplished these three routes upon my destined path but be forewarned, our minds are cluttered, so finding mindfulness in the comfortability of our own clouded mind is a lie.

Sitting in the momentary peace of not being concerned with the world or its feelings upon your way of life is one thing but most assuredly you'll get up to eat, check your email or answer the cellphone and swiftly your back into the world of distractions.

So allow me to reiterate, the mindfulness we seek should be in the mindfulness of Christ; his teachings, his examples and most of all his sacrifice.

This is why wisdom should be relentlessly sought after, for this is the age of mindfulness not the extinction of the mindless.

Now as far as that offer to stay in the realm of enlightenment I spoke on earlier, turns out there's no coming back; at least in the since that was shown to me.

Talk about a serious consequence, either I remained in this place of blissful peace and joy or I immediately return back to the reality of my time upon the earth.

There was no gray matter within the sides, either stay or go; I swiftly chose to leave from this place and remain in the allotted time God gave me with my wife and children.

Know that if this conscious state is ever reached, it's of the will God bestowed upon your soul to decide, so choose carefully.

If you've read my previous book THE CONSCIOUSNESS OF MAN, you'd know how serious I am when it comes to the spiritual travels through dreams; that is the possibility of something other than yourself taking ownership of your temple upon return!

Honestly I don't know If I could have awaken from the dream or not but what I do know is, you cant have this life and the level of enlightenment I was shown at the same time; i'll explain further in future writings.

Moreover, on a lower level of earthly enlightenment, I submitted to God's provisions and mercy.

With this humbleness now obtained, I then sacrificed my total self, mind, body and soul for the unconditional love of my future wife; this means to set aside all doubts or fears and trust wholeheartedly in the Holy Spirit.

In this, I fulfilled the covenant of marriage by the bonding of two held together within the law of our created purposes.

By the both of us becoming one in christ, I then possessed the strength to lay waste to the embedded fears, insecurities and manifested barriers hindering my mind from the awakening of true consciousness.

In this state of presence, knowledge and awareness can swiftly be absorbed.

Now stands a man in complete confidence, humbled as the mindfulness of christ's teachings swiftly enters. In this, he's able to brush away the cloudiness of thought, leaving the canvas of one's mind prepared for the   vividness of wisdom.

This for the preparation of unveiled wisdom through the clouds of deceit, my search turns out to be the journey in and of itself as the experience gained along the path; wisdom is finally revealed.

Now the question is how to live, utilize and abide by it, for whatever is diligently sought after must be carried with great authority.

End route as far as what it took to get me there but for you, God may have a different route; if so follow it in complete obedience.

James 1:5

"If any of you lack wisdom, let him ask of God, that giveth to all men liberally, and upbraideth not; and it shall be given him. " - King James Bible

8 CHAPTER

NO OPINIONS NECESSARY

Stand firm and steady your mind from opinionated concerns! Whether from external or from within, remember you are blessed with a most beautiful peace within your purpose. Know that most perceived images or unwarranted whispers are not usually your own, but rather insidious distractions, embedded for the specific purposes of manifesting doubt.

Upon this doubt naturally births hesitation, within hesitation is an unwarranted life, which often cripples your forward progression. Is it wisdom you seek or the wiles of power? Know the difference for whatever words you lend to the ears of others, being the utter of digression will surely come tenfold within your yield of harvest.

It is at this point when you should hold your tongue, if you're even the slightest of confused. Then immediately stop and take personal inventory of who's speaking around you, persuading or leading your atmosphere.

You'll find the ones closest to you at your time of blindness are also blind, feeding and ushering in the darkness around you.

Simply notice but don't judge, for the negative people in your circle are momentary as well as for your immediate development as a true leader.

Acknowledge that their desire for sensationalistic drama is often satisfied by your pain, verbal tantrums or insecurities; don't vent lest they siphon your life force. Know that every step you take upon the path of righteousness, those of ill intent will closely follow.

They are whimsically drawn to your light in hopes you fail, in this falling back into that deep dark abyss of blind fowls; flocking without flight.

I know it feels good to vent while rhetorically expressing your pain, but know this pain is personal fuel for your spiritual growth, not others envious gluttony of your zeal.

Know that the glutinous nature of the ill-advised is an empty pit, ready to consume all you have to give. Walk away swiftly from the wiles of their temptation; for they've spent time upon your path and will remind you of any weakness in which to lead you astray.

Take back your journey and walk upright in the confidence of your spiritual intuition. Listen for the word of Christ, it remains seeded as that little whisper in your heart.

It's there for your beckoning and will remain and grow louder if you accept it as your own but not for others interpretation.

Be warned, listen as it will guide your steps upon the ground but if you speak in question, the wicked will twist the meanings back to you causing hesitation within your journey.

Please know that there is unimaginable value and blessed purpose in your life but you must bare it, step by step mistakes and all.

Proceed in faith and believe in the blessed purpose of good within your heart; this will lead you as well as others close to you to a paradigm of happiness and abundance. Even if the others start off in denial, they will leave but come back in curiosity of your progression.

They will leave again in their disgust, falling for personal issues in which your to follow but stray not; this is your time as a leader by example; continue on in search of wisdom.

Humbleness is the way, so steady your mind and walk upon the solid foundation already created within your destiny. Do this at your own pace and with the respect for others purposely trying or inadvertently trying to persuade your direction.

It's often the simplest of light that attracts the darkness but remember, light cast no shadow; so there's nothing to hide as you continue on.

Think not of your past mistakes, blunders or failures. Steady as you go on this rocky path, just remember what it took to get you this far.

Remember your embedded strengths, glory be to God's favor and keep moving in the opposite direction from which you came.

Again when confronted with those of misunderstanding, show diligence even if it comes from life's little necessities such as marriage, finance and matters pertaining to your job.

This rocky path in which I speak is of metaphorical nature; applied to that of this century. So let not the distractions fool your mind into that of false perceptions, you are without doubt in a spiritual battle; just remain steadfast as you deal within these current times.

If the distractions become more prevalent, speak to it directly! Let them know that their opinions are duly noted but you are within the favor of God's provisions, held to the most high in his glory.

Then proceed forward, handling all business as the character of God you aspire to be.

This is what leaders do! This is more than just possible, because you're more than a possibility. You are God's created purpose for a reason; which leaves you with no excuse but only result!

Please accept that you are an amazing person, no need for the validations or opinions of others treading the same issues. You are complete, you just need to quiet the chatter and pray in the peace, evoke the silence and rest your query mind.

Take hold of your destiny, for it is blessed upon your wildest dreams! This is why it's so vitally important that you stay focused on your personal dreams, goals and ambitions; hence you'd stray away to the excitement of others influences not meant for your journey.

In this, advice and confirmation will reveal itself by the mindfulness of your temple and the comforter within your journey.

So until the true awakening of your purpose, keep in heart that the naysayers will often and most desperately try to cope in their own way, how to manage your newfound driven purpose.

They'll feel the need to give you their best advice but rest assured it'll sway more so of their own personal opinions and perceptions. Unfortunately, if their words are not of the bible's alignment of Christ's teachings, it will only result in the heaviness of baggage upon your back.

When this comes to pass utilize patience and remain steadfast! Humbly accept the weight of their burden and continue your walk.

Your spiritual legs will only get stronger as you recite the words of God over and over again. Know that as a prudent spirit of wisdom, your body with each step of unwavering purpose, gets closer to that of what you seek.

Do this until they either fall from exhaustion over your commitment to God's glory or they release themselves and willingly join your walk. This resulting in the extension of the ministry; as we've come together as one representing the body of Christ.

Know that even the hardest of hearts has ears in which to receive, while grudgingly holding on the back of a righteous person.

In this matter, only time can tell which is stronger, the legs of the spiritually influenced or the arms of the wicked; desperately holding on without direction.

Fortunately, "time is not of the essence" when on the battlefield of our destined path. In other words, time is more of an afterthought because more importantly, while on this journey, what matters most is the decision to follow God's creation for your life.

So again, keep pressing forward as your legs become stronger and stronger, holding no regard for the failures of trivial beings, desperately trying to hold you back.

When they whisper, let them whisper, it's only their opinions and who's to say what's on their tongue has any real bearing, upon what God has already put on your heart.

Whispers, rumors and gossip are generally quiet for a reason, being anything not worth speaking aloud in the confidence of company, could indicate something more deceitful; hence why most people's opinions are not needed whatsoever!

Discern the difference between opinions, hearsay, gossip, second-hand information, ideas, advice and most of all whispers, again if any doesn't align with the word of God; let them roll off your back like the weary arms of failure.

Please accept into your mental storehouse, that you are an amazing person and that you are magnificently beautiful in many ways! You are of greatness and of perfect purpose as you walk within the pace creatively timed and favored by God.

No matter what your ailments, concerns or issues, walk in this faith consistently! Keep pushing forward as though you've already received in God, what you've prayed for all along, even before you started the journey.

Accept that you are healed, this is why you're continually being tested. Accept that you have great purpose, this is why you're relentlessly tried by nonbelievers!

Trust, if you want the chatter of the naysayers and negatively influenced to stop, all you have to do is stop yourself.

In this you'd succumb to their will, going out for that drink, submitting and immersing yourself into that quiet conversation behind closed doors and before you know it; you're shrouded in the darkness of sin.

Now stumbling again and again, over misguided feet set upon a well traveled path to destruction, Be ready, you are prepared, for upon falling guilt will always try to manifest into your mind looking for weaknesses.

Hold your ground, bring forth your commitment as you are deeply rooted into the soil of your purpose; this is why you should always stand guard at the gates of your mind.

Take note, even in this place there remains the mercy of God, turn back swiftly for there is light still burning in your heart, never to be diminished, never to be forgotten and never consumed in totality by the darkness of despair.

Use this flickering of light to guide you back, use what little warmth cast off from the glimmer of your faith to warm your bones within the coldness of dread. You can and will do this; for you are much stronger and capable than you fully realize!

Within this understanding, no insinuations will mislead your life, no other comments will validate who'd they think you to be. Lastly, no one's opinions will distract your anointed walk in faith. Journey on in peace you amazingly wonderful gift from God.

Go ahead, quiet your mind and listen to your heart, walk at your own spirit filled pace and faithfully step into the glory of your victory. Shhh, you hear that?

The chatter has fallen, indicating the silence within your reward! You've made it this far; no sense in turning back from your destiny!

Lastly, I want to impress upon your mind the impending danger of letting your guard down. At times when submerged within the comfortability of your environment, silence your tongue and swiftly cover your ears.

Remember, this is not the time to try and change, persuade or convince others. Disregard the urge to express the specifics of your destined path, for this will most assuredly create frivolous questions posed to take you far from your intended journey.

The wiles of the wicked are cleverly masked within the good intentions of your closest counterparts; especially if they're not on the same journey in life.

This in no part makes them evil but know, good intentions may not be of God's intended purpose for your overall leadership responsibilities.

Whether those closest to you purposely intend to mislead you, is not the problem. The actual problem relies within the unprotected mind. This open mindedness upon the counsel of others, leads to the susceptibility of your focus.

In this the clever remarks, charismatic ideas and unwarranted opinions from those nearby, has a way of sowing seeds of thorns within your thought process; hence those closest can reveal a weakness in your journey.

Recall the very definition of opinions are of one's personal views or judgement. Furthermore, regarding what they perceive to be truthfulness within their own reality. This goes to say their personal understandings, may have no real bearing based off facts or specialized knowledge.

This issue beckons the question, who's to say another's perception is that of actual truth?

It doesn't make any difference how passionate a lie, misconception or blatant disregard for one's ability to make up their own mind but when construed in the form of opinion; that's where   another's influence becomes a dagger. Again, unwarranted opinions will handicap and expose the weakness of an unguarded mind.

Ready yourself at the gates of your mind, for eventually it connects to the passageway to your heart. Let no other force whisper within the channels of your heart, for in this place far from understanding is a path deeply hidden.

This path in turns reveals the passageway to your subconscious. In this the subconscious is all in what we seek, for in this realm of unimaginable power, relies the unfathomable nature of the comforter herself, better known as the Holy Spirit; it is here where wisdom is found.

1 Kings 18:21

"And Elijah came unto all the people, and said, How long halt ye between two opinions? If the LORD be God, follow him: but if Baal, then follow him. And the people answered him not a word." - King James Bible

9 CHAPTER

KNOW THYSELF

Now that you are well upon this path of staying spiritually focused and just as importantly, remaining a leader by heartfelt example; now is the time to evaluate your position. Understanding who you are will help expedite any changes needed to be revealed prior to creating powerful disadvantages set against your progress.

Understand the stronger you grow the more careful you must become when developing your strengths; lest you'd derail your good efforts for an abomination of ill expectations.

In this paradox of obscurity, one can inadvertently hinder their path, casting good efforts into a down spiral of whimsical denial. In this the true enemy can reveal itself if the traveler is blind to one's true self, which is why it's so vitally important to often take the time to assess, learn and eventually come to know thyself.

Here you'll find the true enemy is not of others ill intents, curse filled thoughts or blatant hatred but rather your own fears, guilt and insecurities.

When this understanding is reached, you can now comprehend in full depth of your mind's capabilities and why only mindfulness in Christ's teachings should be adhered.

Please know that by any other means, mindfulness will not be reached in totality but rather, suffer the ailing fate of one's current misunderstandings of life.

Moreover, the blissfulness of denial achieved, will bring about the absolute failure of sought after wisdom in its entirety. Upon this, leading further into the lessor of any hopeful gains of abundance or happiness once desired. If continued on this path, the overall results will be the likeness of fools lost in their monetary spoils, making a mockery of their true and destined purpose.

Please remember, when the power of changed perception comes to pass, grow with the intellect of God's grace; not the self idolization of one's newly found riches.

Be careful not to alter the path in which originally sought, being deviation from purpose beckons that of temptation. This in which I speak, is the temptation to mingle within the corrupted mindset once condoned within your temple.

It is only in the knowledge gained, which will strengthen your spirit not to turn back into the wilderness of doubt but remain steadfast upon your journey.

This knowledge is acquired from your chosen path of endured pain, as well as your blessed response regarding the naysayers through the toughest of trials.

Your showing of outstanding faith will be rewarded in the revelation, that the evils of hatred, envious of nature and jealous of heart, possess no dominion over your God given created purposes.

Boldly speak into existence this faith and hold dear to your heart, the meek spirit intended to promote you pass the ignorance of the wicked.

Invest love, faithfulness and confidence within yourself by loving our heavenly father, learn and do the will of God, for his best intentions will always be for your blessed benefit.

Never lose your mind in the wilderness of deceit, for in this place relies all that is opposite for your intended good.

Remember this when presented with the gentle kiss of lust, mingle not into this temptation, for it will poison your heartfelt desires of love. Hold tightly within your grasp the aspirations of heart. If lust seeps into its channels, your given dreams become of stone; swiftly casted into a sea of forgetfulness.

Have faith! Know that of mind, body and spirit, you within the faculties of your mind can create a reality of joy, peace and influence.

At any given time within your life, you can choose to be happy, just as you choose with all other accepted emotions.

The only issue is, instead of seeking joy from within, we believe that joy comes from the hetero-suggestions of our world. We, since birth upon this planet have been given just enough education to fit in the status-quo.

This in part, justifies the ease of leading a nation of blind followers, rather than growing each and everyone's spiritual rights of clarified vision.

Here's an example, recently I mentioned "At any given time within your life, you can choose to be happy." It takes a little effort but no more than the effort one achieves by thinking negatively until they themselves become what they've created!

This is, if you focused on a spouse committing adultery, you will most assuredly become jealous. Whether the act was committed or not, your mind thought it to be; resulting in a physical manifestation. The very act of creating the image in mind, tells your subconscious you're being abused, resulting in the neurological feedback that you're physically sick, angered and of jealousy.

Want an even better more practical example? I'll start with a question, can you heal yourself of disease, pain or depression? My answer to this is; YES!

Being I practice positive spirit-filled suggestions daily in conjunction with the teachings of Christ. As far as the practical example,   honestly ask yourself this question and truly ponder the many ways it may have come to reality in your life.

Have you ever thought of a sexual desire so emphatically that you became physically arouse? Have you ever had what was thought to be a nightmare and you awakened cold, jittery and temporarily scared out your mind thinking it was actually real?

How about this one, have you ever made yourself cry by way of purposeful thought, to convince or persuade another that you indeed were hurting in some form or way?

I'm talking real tears, flowing down your face at the mere image of your mind's cognitive ability to express an outward result, even though it wasn't of real nature.

Please don't be stubborn, if you've never conjured up tears, have you ever cried yourself to sleep from fear or worry; what of watching an amazingly beautiful love story? Just know, the images created turned on the emotional faculties of you mind, bringing forth the result of physical waterworks.

These all have in relations the same effect of using your mind's power to achieve a physical result!

Right now, on the spot if you wanted too, you could cause goosebumps to arise somewhere on your body, simply by breathing and invoking thoughts combined.

The reasonings of our embedded powers and strengths are so simple, we again become as blind followers, confused or   better yet; unadulteratedly misinformed.

What I'm saying is most people are in such disbelief of their true potential, they've become blinded by the worldly rhetoric of sensationalism! So much so, they've subjectively accepted the idea, that real power or the like thereof, is obtained within a pharmaceutical drug or that of a Marvel or DC comic book character.

Don't be fooled into thinking you're not special, don't be tricked into thinking you must at all cost, look like a supermodel or physically chiseled athlete. You are not only beautiful beyond measure but such is true of your intellect; if you chose to believe!

Again, believability is king in the temple of one who chooses this faith, in any capacity! What do you believe? Do you believe in God, do you believe in life, do you believe in yourself? All the above should be answered yes!

Simply because, out of over one hundred and fifty-million sperm cells, you were chosen to be born into this reality.

Furthermore, being that you are in fact of this reality, the very essence of the word reality, constitute things that actually exist. This including your physical self, your tangible life and most importantly, your heavenly creator God the almighty.

Now with the knowledge of getting to know thyself a bit more, as well as your life and your creator, understand that we often dumb down the things we don't fully understand.

We've been taught since childhood, if we can't explain it, see it or touch it for scientific explanation; it must not be real. I beg to differ, being that we've accepted that gravity is real even though we can't see it, the air we breathe is obviously real even though we can't walk on it and the spirit of God is real even though we can't touch it.

Here's what's tangible about all three of the examples given, even though only two is really taught in scientific capacity, we can't actually see, stand upon or touch the categorized examples.

Although they all unequivocally possess one physical principle we can't ignore; we can absolutely without any disagreement feel the magnitude of their force.

You can feel the pull of gravity if you'd jumped off a high enough surface, you can feel the coolness of air within an Island breeze pushing your sail abroad and you can profoundly feel the presence of God.

Especially if you were instructed to walk, learn and abide by his word, as often as you were taught about the relationship between air and gravity.

Think about this, what if you believed in the embedded powers of healing, built into your physical and spiritual makeup, just as much as you believed in the oxygenated air you breathe or the law of gravity and its workings.

These are simplistic examples of our belief systems in constant practice. Think about this, everyday we acknowledge, respect and enjoy the principles of the law of gravity as mentioned.

Either by jumping off a diving board, leaping over a puddle after the rain or flying first class in an airplane. All routinely practiced, enjoyed and accepted as a part of everyday reality. The point here being, what we believe in more by way of accepted teachings, trust and faith, will grow and become more of an influence in our present day reality. So what do you believe in more?

The fact that our creator gave us the ability to heal ourselves of any sicknesses, diseases and or depressions or that pharmaceutical conglomerates, carefully constructed a drug for the betterment of our lives?

I pose these questions to shed light on the emphatic answer of YES, as in earlier when I stated the question of believing we can heal from pain, disease or depression.

Again, I impress upon those reading, I answered "YES" because as stated it's a part of my everyday routine, in conjunction with the teachings of Christ. I am living proof, as well as countless others of the abundant life, ushering in health, wealth and spiritual blessings of acquired knowledge.

Please accept, all is possible when immersed within the grace of God's provisions and lastly, take time to access yourself in his word; for this is the only way you can truly learn to know thyself.

1 Timothy 4:7

"But refuse profane and old wives' fables, and exercise thyself rather unto godliness."- King James Bible

10 CHAPTER

COMMUNION OF THE RIGHTEOUS

Let's talk, its time to really open up for the ones who truly seek knowledge in good regard. There is a fine line between sharing information and receiving information and it has something intricately devised to do with the perception of one's true intent.

On the receiver side, getting good information yields great rewards but only if valor was accepted to achieve or to reproduce results from what is actually learned.

In other words information is given, shared and taught to be acted upon, for the betterment of life's philosophies in action.

On the teacher's side, information given, shared and taught comes threefold. One is to provide just enough information to create curiosity in the mind of the receiver, in this the receiver develops a natural desire to seek more information. This for the purposes of merit, factual evidence and greater growth upon philosophy.

Secondly, the teacher again provides just enough information in the capacity for the learned, to give and develop confidence in the form of truth and honor.

In this, there relies the power to push through the difficult times of change, when challenged by forces that seek to destroy good teachings.

Lastly, the teacher who has achieved advanced knowledge understands, that any power misconstrued in the slightest way would unravel the very foundation of our life's purposes. So to balance out this power, the teacher will yet again, only provide just enough to the receiver in which to restore or maintain balance.

In other words, a teacher has many students in which to balance the scales of knowledge, that is if the balance of power is ever corrupted. The wiles of the wicked is always afoot, trying to seek knowledge as well, this is why often you'll hear the phrase "the devil is in the detail."

Know that they of evil doings or intent will submit to the teachers of good, as to learn how to corrupt the power within the teachings. This is why it's so vitally important to seek from within the spirit for direction, confirmation and leadership.

Upon this you'll attract by way of universal law what is good for your growth, abundance and wisdom.

Use this understanding well upon the path of knowledge seeking within the literature of the world; being you'll have to decipher good from evil yourself.

This is why I ask to "be honest," Being I want to commune with you on a spiritual level, within the printed words of this book.

This of course has been done since the days of writing, transmuted into communicative language, so communion with me please.

Time to decipher if I, the author speaks truth from the heart, being I claim to be of an authority on the subject.

I am the teacher claiming to be of advanced knowledge, by way of spiritual influence within the guidelines of the Holy Spirit; which I've come to know as wisdom herself.

I openly submit in totally transparency my intentions of providing truth but as previously stated a "teacher has many students in which to balance the scales of knowledge."So being I've written shared knowledge amongst the masses that would be considered students of acquiring this knowledge, I written in such a way as to balance out the teachings from those that would otherwise corrupt the goodness of purpose.

Simply put, I shared but fragments of seeds in which to manifest truth within your spirit.

In this only you can derive the perfection of God's creation from your life; if you're good at heart. This is why I started with stories, to see if I could strike an accord with one's imagination of real life circumstances.

This is why I've shared hit or miss analogies to awaken your heart once you've crossed certain barriers in life.

For instance, some of what is written will have no bearing on your life until it's been revealed within your own personal vision or dreams. In this the reward depends on the purity of heart invested.

Trust, if certain strengths are meant for you, one day you'll revisit the pages of this book and with absolute clarity you'll confirm truth shared, when at first you couldn't see.

Also, within the pages of this book, I brought forth questions pertaining to this generation in time, for the purposes of addressing current issues of true importance. Not the empty sensationalistic drama, that is the distractions of the world created to pull you into the misguided ways of segregated opinions.

Simply put, we have a much greater purpose other than pointing fingers in judgment of another's doings. In my journey upon finding wisdom, I was shown the differences in people, are not the issues of the world but rather the indifference of knowledge.

In other words, the prudent use of one's theological understandings paired with wisdom, while elevated within the faculties of our minds, has been and will always be under attack; unless we learn beyond the falsehood of corrupted influences.

The differences within myself, is how I've perceived the world to be upon my time within this realm.

All physical and mental forces within the environment, my cultural upbringings and traditions are added to the inner workings of what is the makeup of my soul.

Remember the soul is the harmonious moral and emotional connection within our body, as it relates to the eternal spirit.

In other words, what we believe the soul to be is the equivalent of what our brain is to that of our hearts. Ponder this comparison if confused, don't just take my word on it; research for yourself.

Here's a little thought process to get you started, does your brain actually do the thinking or does your heart, maybe it could be the mind? Even though the heart has millions upon millions of neurons, more than that of our brains, we often still think in contrast.

Your brain in representation of your mind, as the heart is to your spirit.

Even though the latter of both organs represents something more than physical anatomy, one must consider the source of power relies elsewhere as a form of communication between the physical and spiritual world.

Most have come to accept that their brain holds the process of the mind, so when a person ventures to concentrate, they tend to put their hands on their head and squint your eyes closely shut. Focusing on the mental image of your brain, reaching out through your body to connect or withdraw what is at that point most desired.

If this is true, why when we suddenly get caught off guard or surprised, we immediately put our hands on our heart; not our heads? Why do we cuddle and embrace by bringing our hearts closer to each other in a time of comfort or need. Just know that the brain, as important as it is pertains more to the physical motor skills of the body pairing up with the cognitive ability of our minds.

Lastly, why when we're in love, in hurt or in the insatiable desire to help others do we feel it in our hearts; far before our minds adds its options of matter?

Who's to say your appendix doesn't hold many more key factors but honestly, we weren't taught much on this part of the anatomy. This aforementioned of "matter" that is our brains, holds the sum total of our experiences and perceived understanding since birth, which is the makeup of what we've come to believe is our soul. You've heard of the connection between mind, body and soul right?

This is why the soul is separate from the eternal spirit which God created within our subconscious. Although, soul can be interchangeable with the word spirit, depending on the person's intent or definition of term.

Either way, its up to you to find the wisdom for yourself if you truly want the power in the understanding to be released in you.

Here's something else I'd like to share, the old image of the devil or the like thereof, fabricating a physical contract, such as in cartoons, behind closed doors or in movies since our childhood, is simply wickedness at work.

If you allow these images to manifest into your mind, upon adulthood you'll come to believe that sins cannot be forgiven, lies cannot be untold and guilt cannot be erased.

In other words, giving in to the "spirit" of failure, upon the imperfections of what it is to be human, is a deception to those seeking God's overall purpose for our lives.

Know that if the opposer can get you to believe that you're not worthy, by way of guilt or any other depressing thought; this image will turn to a burden.

A burden so thick with clutter, it will diminish the light that dwells within your body, mind and soul.

Again, although your "soul" cannot be bargained for, the corruption of it can have devastating effects within the subconsciousness of your mind and being what relies in this place is eternal, you might want to stand guard even more so at the entrance of your mind.

Once again I must reiterate, the image of bargaining through a blood oath, by way of signature on a dotted line, for the opposers intent of forever owning your soul is a lie, let this image go. Your worldly created idea of soul, is not your eternal spirit. "It" that is the eternal spirit, belongs to the creator which is God.

Remember hat which is in you, is of his image and in this, is the sealed salvation ransomed by the resurrection of Jesus Christ. Nothing of this earth or the realms that be, can take what God has given.

With this said, now consider your brain in representation of your mind, as the heart is to your spirit. Then regard these physical attributes as vessels for much needed understandings. Even though the latter of both organs represents something much more than physical anatomy, one must consider the source of true power lies elsewhere.

With this knowledge, will you research science for ways to rape the natural laws set in place or will you decipher the living word of God, as to reveal the means of your power already bestowed within your subconscious?

Either way a balance is in place for good to prevail, so if your goal is to find wisdom, remember it already resides within you as the comforter.

How you interact with it, depends on the very essence of your hearts desires. Find your confidence and invoke your faith, do this without the world's influence and what you truly seek will be revealed.

A word to the wise, what you think, focus or mentally conjure up will have the root effect in your reality. Know thyself, be honest with yourself and others. Lead and be humble in the manner and truth of purpose will be yours to yield.

If not apparent, let's quickly go through the steps of this book and see if there is a pattern, that'll help enlighten your journey as you seek what is yours to find.

First was to embrace the steps of isolation, in order to face and conquer our fears upon the journey; this is the a walk of purpose.

Secondly, understanding our perceptions of life, is not the same as life itself. This revealed that under the natural law of free will, our sense of mindfulness is flawed.

Then on to focusing your strengths in order to find complete awareness of one's self. This in turn lead to the traditions of shared knowledge passed down through the ages as in the sands of time.

By the time these efforts are upheld, experience would have been gained, leading to the acquired knowledge reminding us not to become judgmental.

Furthermore into the journey, we uncover the shadow of an object, is not the object itself but only the likeness of the object.

Then on to the difficulties of enlightenment and chosen routes for achievement, bringing to light the courage needed to press on through the distractions. By now, stopping to evaluate one's self is key to the development of revealed understandings.

Those in which would usher in truth, within embedded powers of faith, will in fact do so if honestly believed. Then lastly, communion with the servant of righteousness, in order to receive what one truly deserves for services rendered upon the journey.

Psalms 37:4

"Delight thyself also in the LORD; and he shall give thee the desires of thine heart."

-King James Version Bible

THE HIDDEN CHAPTER

THE LONG WALK

This book is a tool for awakening the mind to acquire wisdom in an age of informational overload, overstimulation and complacency.

The acquisition of wisdom is for the purposes of navigating through life with the fullest of joyful experiences, peace and happiness. This means, although there are many worldly subjects of interest created to pull and fragment our intended purposes, we must remain spiritually whole to uphold the natural laws set in place for our purpose.

Take the mighty tree for example, it follows the natural purpose of God's created intention. From seed it grows into its fullest potential, without concern of the outside world. Its height, shade and fruit will be given unto the earth until it returns to the soil.

This is the purpose of life but as human beings we question the "purpose of life," as if we would earnestly follow the natural universal orders of God's laws intended.

Actually what's happening is when a person is unsatisfied with their personal path or choices in life, they ask "what's the meaning of life?"

In hopes they'd get an easy answer, in which to derive what's pliable to their wellbeing and disregard the difficulties conducive to personal desires.

If they'd be like the mighty tree completely unselfish within itself, bearing fruit and providing unbiased sheltered for those in needs, life would be much fulfilled and in rarity of thoughtless wonder.

I understand that humans are vastly different from trees but the example remains steadfast. We were created for very specific purposes, in which to thrive within our environment. If one ask what is this purpose? I'll again use the analogy of the tree and explain why analogies often work better than straight answers .

The tree bears its fruit upon the land as mankind bears their children upon the world. The tree provides shelter throughout the seasons of nature, mankind creates shelter within the elements of this nature.

Lastly, the tree in the height of its fullest maturity, stretches its limbs to the heavens and gives back its essence through the winds of change, man yields his life's work with withered hands to the winds of time.

Both in their allotted time on earth, will serve a purpose within the natural laws of life. Only difference is how we as human beings choose to live our lives.

Since man is born of free will, there relies the bombardment of his continuous thought process. The relentlessness of his thoughts, often brings about frivolous questioning.

These bewildered questions sanctions the intake of unmerited ideas, opinions and perceptions. All in the name of much sought after answers, that is until the comfortability of one's personal liking is accepted.

The reason why analogies are often better than straightforward answers are, most people already know the answer by way of gut feeling or intuition. It's just that the differences between right and wrong are so unambiguous, the cluttered mind requires time to cope and adjust to the truth.

What better way than to offer the warmth of story, while easing the overstimulated mind. In this, creating colorful images of reasoning in simplistic form and transforming thought into a personal experience.

Remember what the mind thinks, the subconscious brings forth by way of physical manifestations, in other words our feelings. This is why movies, music and literature are so vitally important to the body.

Simply put, it draws you in the realm of the story and what better way to compare the likeness of what's seemingly different, to that of God's universal laws for all forms of his creation. For all that has life, nourishes the embedment of seed for the continuation of life itself.

With this said, we actually have the ability to acquire a piece of heaven on earth, by way of God's intended purpose for our lives.

Again, this reflects on how we choose to live our lives while navigating through the essence of life itself.

All this, within our accepted ideas and perceptions gained along the chosen path.

Now upon being confronted with the simplicity of truth, most people circle back to square one! That is their unappeasable desire to seek the personal fulfillment of informational change, which lures and over stimulates the mind in hopes to find rest within the satiety of complacency.

Now as far as my knowledge upon the matter, it's often effortless to give straightforward advice, especially since it's a book offering that of wisdom.

Only the very essence of spiritually gained wisdom, requires that either you traverse in similarity of my footsteps, or commune within the analogies of my learned experiences.

It's often accepted that one's acquired knowledge on a particular subject or expertise, is based off the works of other literature, scrolls, experiences and even ancient documentation. Whether it's readily available sources of information or systematically release knowledge of cloaked provisions.

All that is written or expressed in matter of literary content, will always be traced back to that of someone's personal experiences.

This is true to great extent and since I've matched my life's trials with biblical scriptures, it is my purpose for you to see how we all relate through the teachings of Christ.

Know that the predominance of stories in this book comes from spiritual guidance gained through personal trials, visions and circumstances.

This is why I research the bible, its history and purpose for the betterment of purpose.

Clearly this was no easy task, being the knowledge gained required much diligence. Trusting in visions and dream are difficult at first but when confirmed by way of biblical scripture and real life circumstances, one comes to the realization that there is no doubt a higher power at hand.

Accepting the parables and analogies of the bible, are meant for us all to look deeper into the scriptures.

This bringing the hope that you'd uncover, realize and fully understand the answers sought after.

It is my purpose to correlate everyday life circumstances to that of solved principles through scripture. In this, learning an acquired amount of wisdom through the experiences of biblical reference will be more beneficial to your journey.

Within the communion of spiritual influences in your life, whether good friend, mentor or trusted confident, confirmation by way of research will help cleanse the cluttered mind, allowing for the embedment to be released from your subconscious.

In this hidden chapter, I'll give a working example on how the use of wisdom, can guide your steps in a time of absolute attack. Again, it's considered effortless to just give advice but in the next few paragraphs, I'll walk you through a physical and mental battle that changed the course of my life as a young adult.

You want to acquire wisdom? This is what it looks like applied in today's generational circumstances. See yourself within the footsteps of my journey, as it may help you through your trials, that is if ever challenged on a level I suffered.

While upon this walk of transparency, try to visualize and ask yourself, what would you have done in my circumstance.

Understand, I had no mentor, friends or family to lean on. No human spiritual advisor and even more importantly, no outlets regarding escape. The outlets in which I speak are on any level pertaining to that of adultery, alcohol, drugs, violence or any other mental stimulation, that would otherwise create temporary escape from the pain. Again, ask yourself being totally honest, what would you do?

As a young man in my early twenties, anxious in my desire to do more than what was culturally expected, I was closer than ever to reaching a goal of personal achievement.

It was three years in the making, sweating away in the back of a hot restaurant full of bigotry and prejudice. Apparently, I was the only black person with the tolerance to stay in this environment but I had a gridlocked purpose and finally I was close to achieving my hearts desire.

From a dishwasher that wasn't allowed to show the darkness of his skin, to that of a line cook was considered an exceptional achievement in my understanding.

Even in my most humble attempt to recollect, I can't actually say that from the mop bucket, to pantry, then on to broiler cook and sauté position was easy but I can say, the knowledge acquired from the master chef was well worth the weight in gold.

As the pummeling of racist remarks were the practice of routine, I recall only one person ever asking 'how can you take them saying "nigger go-fer this or f-ing nigger go-fer that!? He nor they, had the slightest idea that the oppressions of the kitchen, paled in comparison to my actual life at home.

If you're starting to sway to the imagery, that this is a suppressed story concerning my experiences with racism; please don't. This will only bring about blockages, formed from personal or media influenced propaganda, created for opinionated resolve.

In short, pulling you from the truth within the underlying story of acquiring wisdom and back into the distracting issues of the world.

Even though the oppressing of my rights, while being labeled as the scapegoat of all that was wrong within the black community was their norm, let me ease the idea by submitting no, I had deeper ditches to climb out. This is just the beginning of what is needed to acquire an ear for wisdom, so again please do not fall for personally embedded distractions.

Something of greater spiritual importance is within these paragraphs; hence the hidden chapter. Now back into my shoes, this part of the day was the easiest of my walk, being I balanced their bigotry with my centered attention on memorizing and taking notes from the mastery of this chef abilities.

Little did he know I was studying the means to culti-vate my own personal escape through the culinary artistry of food. Now moving back to that anxious day of achievement, I recall the nervous excitement upon my heart. I remember kissing the cheeks of my first born and baby girl with a promise, prior to having the door slamming swiftly behind me.

No stress, I knew today had to be the day of promo-tion, being the chef asked me to come in early to prep for the sauté station.

All I could think of at the time, was when I returned home later that night, I was going to announce to her my culinary achievement but before this was to happen, I had to traverse the nearly thirteen mile walk to the restaurant.

On to the pavement I stepped with an upbeat rhythm, confident in my abilities to achieve what I knew I've earned in the years of sweat and toil. Only this feeling of unstop-pable swagger was short lived just as soon as my stride be-gan. At this moment I was drawn to the thumping base of music, blaring from a certain car creeping down my street.

Boom-boom-ba-boom! As the vibration of the loud base rattled the windows of parked cars nearby. All I could think was "please don't let this guy slow down, please lord, just let him keep driving." But that wasn't the case, some-how the neighborhood drug dealer got word I was on my way to work; Boom-Boom-ba-Boom creeping louder!

As the candied painted monstrosity slowed but not to a complete halt, I glared at his window as if I could actually see through the tint. Dread seeped into the pit of my stomach as the brake lights brightened just a bit.

I knew he was waiting for me to turn the corner and even though my pace slowed to a stop, I couldn't help but momentarily stand there like an idiot reciting to myself, don't do this reggie she's been clean now for two months.

Insecurities flooded my mind, why was I so frail in spirit? I've survived helping her through rehab, the courts system and countless times of domestic abuse and there is no way she'd throw it all away. Not now, not with me becoming all that I've worked so hard to achieve. Boom-boom-ba-boom! Again, as the thundering base of his speakers wreck my concentration.

Boom-Boom-ba-Boom as I allow the devil to pounced upon my shoulders and in to my mind, whispering "that's why she was so fidgety, rushing you out the house!"

Get behind me Satan! I screamed to myself while forcing my legs to proceed forward. One stumbling foot in front of the other, pushing onward in hopes of making the end of the street.

Such as the perception of life, just as I was turning that dreaded corner, his brake lights burst into a bright solid glimmer. That bastard stopped no sooner than I turned.

My legs went numb, I started to feel as if all eyes were on the stupidity and cowardice of my decision.

Again, Just keep moving I thought to myself, whether people of my neighborhood knew the intricacies or not. In this, I knew this was a battle and I couldn't let fear take over my mind. But what can a man do in the weakness of his insecurities?

Hurt and embarrassed, filled with low self-esteem and broken understandings. What can a man do? Was this an embedded act of spiritual bravery or was it an act of manifested cowardliness? This all in hopes to avoid facing my fears of a relationship in absolute turmoil.

Even with each step facing the likelihood of derogatory insults from my job, I stuttered no more and relentlessly pushed forward. It's going to be fine I tried to convince myself, It's going to be ok and for a moment the further I walked away, the less of an embarrassment I felt but of course this didn't last for long.

Again, the fear of the mind kicks in, telling me "I could take him out and no one would care, just another drug dealer lost to the streets!"

Even worse, I knew where that skinny rat lived and "it wouldn't be the sweat off my bow to end his life," but really, was I going to become a murderer?

No, not to justify the ailment of the woman's addiction to crack cocaine; even if she was at the time my wife. In this case, I'd dare not leverage my children's future over her relapse to addiction, a drug dealer or my insecurities.

No, because nothing would come out of it but the lure of her temptation desperately seeking a fix. Not to mention my children would grow up knowing their father was in prison; fitting the cultural stereotype so well accepted in my generational upbringing.

No doubt a win-win for the devil and the corrupted powers that be, being I would have fit right in, as another black male imprisoned for life as a murderer, drug dealer or thief. All titles accepted under the workings of the wicked.

No! I affirmed to myself, just keep walking! Not to forget, I couldn't be late in the absolute fear that I'd be fired on the spot.

"Just keep moving Reggie," something within my heart pleaded with me, "let them laugh, let them snicker and eventually let them go!" As tears begin to pour down my cheek, I felt like I was dying with every step.

By now within the weakness of my spiritual immaturity, I allowed the devil to attack again and again. This time with even more vivid images of this drug dealing-rat, doing things to her sexually as for payment, I'd never do in my most lustful state, being this was the woman I vowed my hand in marriage.

To death do us part, through sickness and health and for better or worse, I had a bigger purpose. All I had to do was to take this spiritual beating and just keep on walking.

Pain, pain, excruciating pain, like a burning jagged knife ripping down into my chest. Pain and even more again, with a feeling of no end in sight but nevertheless, I continued on with every step. Passerby's look with curiosity upon my tormented face, obviously I must have worn it loudly upon my walk.

Either way I had to move on, hoping that when I got home, she'd at least scamper around the house in a frenzy, pretending she didn't know what happened to the VCR, jewelry or valuables.

Of course by this time, I'd succumb to the probable and accepted, that her giving the drug dealer anything of my household belongings, was better than my wife selling her body to the impotence of a drug pushers fallen purpose in life.

In this understanding, this drug dealing rape-artist was no different from any other form of wickedness birth from evil intent.

This would include adultery, whether by addiction or not, the hate of the street's growing more offensively to my understanding and even the subjection of working for a racist boss.

All is game in the eyes of evil but how could I avoid the causation of turmoil developing in my heart? It's simple to accept when others say "let go and let God," but honestly what does that mean, when all you truly hear is the boisterous screams of agony ripping through your brain.

Needless to say, the day pressed on, the shift was over and the sauté position was mine. Freedom in a sense as I leave the restaurant physically yet mentally exhausted, now readying my mind for the long walk home. With no surprise, as the crisp of wind in the dark of night hits my face, I find myself immediately fighting the battle within the mind. Only now with renewed and clearly refreshed images of insecurities, growing and taunting my every step.

Childish as my undeveloped mind attacks my thought process, foolishly regurgitating the sickness of my lustful teenage years. Ignorant thoughts now applied to my life in a way a healthy mind would never fathom. Whether true or not, fact or fiction the thought was created.

Moreover, years upon years, the seed of wickedness manifested inwards, finally comes full circle in my latter-years; haunting me immensely.

Then unexpectantly, a peace comes over my weathered body, like a cool breeze in the heat of night, reminding me "all I need do is to follow God's will, not the will of man."

THE BOOK OF WISDOM

By now I was at the threshold of my home, miles upon miles walked in the matter of what seemed to be seconds. Where did the time go or better yet, where did my mind wander? Still to this day, I can't positively recollect but that's fine, the end result was of good doings.

As I entered my house, my wife at the time was asleep, nothing of material value appeared to be given or missing.

I didn't bother to wake her in hopes of sharing my new position at work. My little ones were barely up, cuddling on the couch waiting for daddy to come home.

As I marveled upon the blessings of my children's faces, a praise of thankfulness overcame my heart. Moments afterwards, I sat down besides the little joys of my life and as promised, quietly whispered into their ears, daddy's personal achievement at work before falling into a deep, much needed rest.

Thinking back, whether it was love or responsibility, she was still the woman who bared my children, the woman I claimed to love and the woman I vowed in marriage to hold stronger than any personal mishaps awaiting along our journey.

Only this is easier said than done, especially at the start of a relationship when two imperfect, unaware people come together with absolutely no clear understanding of life and what it takes to uphold.

Again in hindsight, was this journey all about the trials of marriage or more so, connecting and strengthening my relationship with God for a much greater task for the future.

It was 17 years later when divorce turn to be absolutely inevitable and still today, I dare not blame my ex-wife for the pain, misery and turmoil faced, bled upon and relentlessly dealt with. Why? Because consequence is the end result of choice and in all that we do as humans, choices are something we've learn to accept.

Can you find the wisdom in this story? You may not feel to the degree I felt upon the long walk, but the wisdom gained from the experience, should be just enough to see the result of God's grace, overall purpose and mercy for our lives.

This walk opened a channel of wisdom, courage and strength thought never to exist, until I challenged the walk. This was only one of many walks but ask yourself, are you open to trust in the lord when you're feeling down and out, gearing up for a walk of your own?

Are you willing to take the higher road in the face of adversity, humbling yourself for others in faith that all is in God's hands? If so, then you are ready to receive the wisdom of life, readily available upon the terrains of your most difficult journeys.

Believe it or not, this story isn't all about me, not anymore in the understanding that, I've developed into what God created me to become, not the lost soul of a man at the beginning of his journey.

This story is more about you and how my journey reflects your current spiritual understanding of forgiveness.

In other words, can you forgive the drug dealer as I did years ago? Turns out that God dealt with him in a way I could have never dreamed! Years afterwards he ended up having kids of his own, got in a church and became a viable member.

His kids grew up and my goodness they are so beautiful, well educated and a wonderful-blessed addition to society. Who was I to have ever thought, I could end a life that God created for a purpose. He was just as lost to the streets, as I was in a marriage I didn't belong.

As for my ex-wife, I forgave her as well, in fact over and over again for the many issues that followed. Turmoils I still today haven't fully opened up about but she is forgiven.

Truly I thank God for her and the giving birth of my first three amazingly wonderful children! How about my racist boss the master chef?

What he put me through was enough to have any man, from any race, color or creed jump off a building in hopes of ending it all but he as well was forgiven.

Why? Because Christ has forgiven me! Between all that offended me during the long walk, I was the common denominator, I was the link between the dealer, the adulterer and bigot. I was the one, that by "choice," turned from what God was telling me to do as a young man, to trying to construct a life from my own free will.

This is why I thank Christ for leaving us the Holy Spirit. It was the wisdom within her voice that kept my legs moving, willed me to learn from a man of hatred and ultimately defeat the enemy created from within.

Again, my transparency, pain and humility is just the tools used to reflect who you are, right now in your current state. Can my story actually change you? I'd hope so but probably not, being to you it may be as the spectator looking through the glass but the parable still remains.

Can you forgive? Can you forgive yourself? Are you currently going through a walk of your own?

However you answer these questions, know that to desire wisdom is to desire to uphold yourself to a higher purpose while going through.

Do this even if you cant see the silver lining through the thickness of deceit, denial or depression. Trust in God whether you see the end goal or not.

You, I and all are one within the journey of life. So lets share, received and confirm with one another as we journey the walk of life together.

Again, for clarity's sake, can you find the wisdom in this story? Or was it just another story shared and received, in hopes of taking you off your personal life's stressors? Is there a protective barrier shielding your way of understanding or discovering within yourself, the wisdom layered within these last few paragraphs?

The answer depends on what level of consciousness you're in at this present time of life.

Know that reading as opposed to actually experiencing the pain acquired from my walk, is far from truly understanding what I went through, how it hurt me and how It became the precursor to that of wisdom.

You've been hurt before right? Maybe not on the same level but if your as human as I'd like you to be, you're either hurting, been hurt or unknowingly hurting someone else. In this, just ask yourself what have you learned from the experience? How are you learning? Who are you learning from and what is being done to course correct while learning through the experience?

For those that truly seek wisdom, understand that it could take sixteen years, ten years, maybe a few months or even within a matter of a few seconds. Understand the level of depth requiring one to receive wisdom depends solely on the person accepting the truth.

I endured seventeen years of turmoil because I was in denial, co-dependent and an enabler. I advise, implore and plead unto you, don't take as long as I did to open up to the word of God.

In this, know that my mind was so clutter with mess and confusions, I couldn't find the cognitive space within my head to absorb what was needed to change my perceptions. In this form of darkness, at any time I could have lost my mind, my life and my eternal destination.

This is why I forgive, this is why I trust in God and for the purposes of communion with you, is why I write. This is why stories are shared, taught and passed down within analogies and parables. In this with faith that one day, someone of need can utilize knowledge shared to traverse through their own journey.

Matthew 6:15

"But if ye forgive not men their trespasses, neither will your Father forgive your trespasses."

- King James Version

11 CHAPTER

ENTER THE TRUTH

When wisdom is entered into the process of making choices, we become aware of the subtle difference between choice and decision.

Both are very similar in meaning but when the wisdom of light sheds upon the two, the weight in severity cast a much different shadow. Upon the shadows of our mindset, reflect the consequences of acceptance and here is where sheer will directs our course in life.

For example, our minds are more susceptible to the outcome of taking chances as opposed to making informed decisions.

Let's break this down a bit. Making a choice is often in terms of something quick and less decisive, reflecting more on the likelihood of just "taking a chance" on the short term. When one ponders on making a choice, it's often between one or more visually acceptable options.

Should I turn left or right to either fill up on gas or should I go straight home and just relax?

Both mental questions already have a predestined vision, accepted outlook or applied version.

The visual outcome of getting gas or going straight home is far from being detrimental. Which in this case, no stress factor renders an afterthought worth the worry of consequence.

Simply put, a short term fix to an end resolve, is based solely on the ease and comfortability of one's choice.

Now regarding the previous chapter on my first marriage, I made that choice not pondered for the complexity of the long term but more so, a quick fix to a mental nagging of unfocused right from wrong. How does this apply to our everyday lives? Most choices from the mind of the inexperienced, are made from that "quick-fix" mentality, not to forget other peoples opinions and lastly, the ease of one's own cluttered conscious.

This is why we shouldn't lean on our own understanding until mindfulness within a higher consciousness is reached. Again, the mindset in which I speak is in the bible based teachings of Jesus Christ.

Only in this, can one truly ponder what is good for the spirit. I want to express this time and time again, just how important the concept of spiritual growth is in ones journey throughout life.

Regarding my thought process over the years, it was worrisomely amazing, how so many people look for the easy way out of what is meant to make them stronger. But isn't that what we naturally do as human beings?

Moreover regarding the brain and our way of auto-suggested understanding, like the fluidity of water do we seem to strive, fight and conceive of ways to find the path of least resistance?

In the majority sense, yes but there will always come a time in one's life when the inevitable happens; that is change.

In any fashion through the trials of circumstance, change will reveal who we truly are by way of personal choice of action. If no action has taken place, one's progress will be stagnated at best. In this, the inevitability of change will cause frustration, behavioral inconsistencies and cognitive clutter.

This is where the path of least resistance can become a nightmare. Being this lack of understanding sheds light to ones poor mindset in making even the simplest of choices plausible.

In this, is where truth needs to be inserted. Truth in the wisdom of understanding that choices regarding change, requires the diligence of honest thought; here's where the art of informed decision making comes into play.

How can a clouded mind see through the thickness of ones on corruption? In this, decision making will be far from desired results ones requires when the winds of time reveals that change is the only way.

We as mankind may naturally desire the easy way of things but the outcomes of quick frivolous thinking reveals the difficulties created, as circumstances we shun from in life.

When this happens, again comes the consequences of the frustrations, behavioral inconsistencies and cognitive clutter I mentioned earlier.

The truth in this matter is, we create the problems we're so willingly blame on life itself.

It's that desire to flow down the path of least resistance in hopes of acquiring positive resolve but this hope is of denial. A deeply embedded sense of purpose, that can best be described as a foolish act of spiritual selfishness.

In other words, when one denies the truth in created purpose, they submitting to that of lackadaisical thinking. This creates the punishment of mind, solidifying a foundation of mental imprisonment, resulting in the subjection of what's required for enjoying life as God intended.

Here's where the paradox of understanding the mind, making choices and applying informed decisions, by way of mindfulness reveals itself. One cannot seek within the darkness, what one is actively trying to keep hidden!

Hiding from the truth, hiding from making the right choices and ultimately, attempting to hide from the life-giving reasonings of Christ's teachings.

This is why the masses will flee to any other means or alternative path, that promises freedom from the punishment of sins, freedom from the persecution of one's consciousness and again, the mindfulness of selfish intent.

This is the very essence of denial on a spiritual level. To waste consciousness, time and God giving purpose on other means of finding oneself, is the blatant lie holding wisdom captive behind the bars of self-solidified imprisonment.

We know the truth, we know what is required for us from within but oh the sweet indulgence of the flesh.

This desire to be alive, freely driven to break all the rules and to appease whatever comes across our mental or physical temptations, are the very mindsets that beckons the consequence of bitter truth.

Like a child in need of parental guidance, we as children of God need to put our issues of self-fulfillment away and grow into the fulfillment of life's true purposes.

To love, trust, share, give, help, reproduce and praise over and over again; enriching the earth as to remain fertile in the harvest of peace.

This is the wisdom of truth, the wisdom of sacrifice and the wisdom of embedded potential. No other use of wisdom, will produce the life giving result as the essence in truth, any other intention or misuse will yield only the consequence of failure.

This is why all that is done within the darkness of our minds, actions or intentions will eventually be revealed in the light of truth.

We know this by way of good bible based teachings but also we know it by the embedment of intuition, consciousness and the little life examples of universal laws time and time again.

Intuition in the mist of guilt, speaks loudly from the heart and often course corrects the intention before the negative action takes place. Within consciousness, the double negative of almost always, rationalizes weather one can get away with the negative intent.

With this, taking the chance is balanced as acceptable, even though the last thing the mind wants is to get caught.

Either way, the truth of light will come and depending on the heart of the deceiver, one will have no choice but to accept the consequence revealed.

Here's another example of light coming to pass as a universal law, is that of the darkest of night before the day, the rainbow after the storm and even the birth from mothers womb unto this world of limited understanding.

Again we know the truth, we expect it, we strive and desire it as confirmation of the life process. In every sense, the human condition will continue to press on until the consequence of light is shed. Whether in goodness or guilt, purposeful intentions or adolescence mistakes, the truth will always be present here and forevermore.

Here's the greatness in what we do as humans, we don't give up. We're created to survive and survival is what we do best, regardless of how mundane the world appears at any given time.

The war has been won, heaven prevails and all that remains is the earth, toying the ability to have a little piece of heaven while we breathe in the essence of life.

In this age of seeking mindfulness, we will continue on as we do. Exploring new paths, making mistakes and of course gaining experiences along the way.

Here's the good news, out of all the chaos and distractions, more and more people are being touched by wisdom. In this, called by the anointing of the eternal spirit and reborn within the word of God.

My prayer for all that seek knowledge upon this journey, is to try and enjoy the process. Acknowledge the many blessed examples given in life.

Spend more time focusing on goodness and the ability to help others. Love every opportunity and be of joyful representation of the good in people.

Know that when speaking of wisdom regarding the past, it resembles that of a different kind of language. It's no wonder why excerpts from proverbs and other written works of spiritual literature, speaks in a language that personifies the past era.

Stories of the prudent man, the lusting of a mistress, seductive lips of honey, a kiss leading to damnation and the search or lust for gold in greed, is just few of many. Although the past speaks differently, the root of the consequences remain the same, right from wrong and the vastness between good and evil.

Present day wisdom speaks also but often gets muddled in the loudness of the world.

Not to forget, todays relentless push to introduce more and more miseducation and confusions, meant to undermine the clarity of spiritual thought.

Please become aware of deeply seeded clever attacks or distractions such as look here, look here, new evidence recently discover!

Foolish notion such as Jesus may not have been a benevolent supernatural being but rather an alien from another planet with super powers of ancient knowledge!

Look here, look here! A new cave in some foreign country was recently stumbled upon and from the carvings on the wall, actually shows benevolent beings from space, mating with earthly women; creating powerful mutants and so on!

Again, anything that can derail, distract or devalue the wisdom within the bible, will be pressed upon mans cognitive ability to comprehend. This all in hopes of exercising his intimate desires, to exploit the lust of finding a loophole in the word of God.

Before long what will happen is, people will become so fed up with miseducation, unrealized dreams and the overstimulation of guru's and online get rich courses, they will soon digress into that of wanting to just shrivel up and disappear; hence the searching for the mindfulness of self comfort.

Please know, that for our future's sake within this reality, we are not God! We are his children given special abilities and powers within life.

This makes us humans with an eternal connection to the source, not God's ourselves! The introduction to such thinking causes the mind to lose oneself in denial and eventually to that of an idolized narcissistic personality.

No matter what the world wants people to think, the falling into denial of self awareness and becoming your own idol, while worshiping personal success, is nothing more than a waste of life's true purpose.

Creating your own sense of worth, power and respect has nothing to do with the love of others!

Be careful of words and media limiting your thought process to that of lusts. Even trusting the digital world and it's purposely constructed algorithm, in which to lead you to their created idea of what's best suited for you, is a form of accepted denial as well.

When speaking on the media, beware of pseudo meanings leading to the fall of literature as we know it. Including physical libraries and actual books.

If this was to happen, gone will be the days when a parent can sit besides their child and read from the physical properties of a book. Gone would be the memories of campfire stories and reading bedtime stories fulfilling the mind with good content.

That may seem extreme but notice how telephone books have become door stoppers or paper weights.

Most businesses are asking to go paperless, that is until they'll ask no more being the direct deposit of your worth becomes part of everyday transaction.

THE BOOK OF WISDOM

Hopefully we'll always have the ability to argued a bill, being we have a physical receipt in the grip of our hands.

I wonder if most will one day entrusted all their permanent understandings, literature or belief system to that of controlled content.

Fortunately for myself it's not a real concern, being I understand it's just part of the frivolous thoughts I spoke of earlier.

I just want people to come to the realization that we are connected by way of the subconscious, wisdom and strength but this will not be so if we're against each other in thought.

Until the dreams and positive ambitions of people become awaken, sharing truths and stories as information, will always be prevalent and for overall good. If we don't try and find a way to become peacefully connected, forces will continue to separate us.

Maybe it has already started? Ask yourself, does your computer or cellphone take you away from those closest, in hopes of bringing you closer to those far away?

Have we become distant from pure thought or the desire for interpersonal communication? In this, maybe a balance will soon arise to shift our minds back unto the righteous path. Imagine a time with no secrets, no denial and no technology.

Doesn't seem possible I know but maybe something of the sort is already arising within the distractions to balance the loss of human connection.

Let's ponder this for a moment, maybe one day the over-stimulation of controlled telecommunication will subside as a sudden necessity.

Dwindling down as the higher of consciousness starts to grow within mankind. Maybe a day will come when communicating with others by way of telepathic clarity, within the connection of the subconscious, will be revealed once again.

I know, doesn't seem possible but true with all universal laws, a balance with be upon us and good will prevail. So good by to the cell phones and any other matter of digital mayhem used to keep us apart. Moreover, completing the fall of hijacked neurons, cell phones and any form of transmitting devices that would contribute to the enslavement of our consciousness.

The only ones still using the internet or telecommunication devices, will be that of the mentally lost or spiritually corrupted.

If this was to come to pass in our lifetime, the soul of man will grow strong within the mind and the evil thereof will be forced to show their faces.

In this, ultimately launching a worldly attack on those that are not connected to the devices of the world. Labeling all that proclaim to be of higher consciousness as a threat and terrorist's of life.

Feeble as the attack would be, mankind will prevail but not without an uprise so large evil will go back into hiding, waiting to strike its final blow.

By this time something special will come to pass, like a thief in the night, saving us all from the opposing of life's universal laws.

This of course will not come unchallenged by the wickedness of the world, being its might and defenses will be stringently focused on the air.

Preparing to launch upon the media influenced alien intruder, instantaneously appearing before all of mankind within a cloud. In this, all of wickedness will be defeated upon the clarity of a trumpet. Finally revealing the truth of prophet, in that no weapons formed against shall prosper.

Whoa! How did we get to this point? We were just pondering the fall of human connection by way of the distraction of mind.

Either way, no matter what our level, thought or plan of destination, we are all on this path together. Still looking for wisdom?

Know this and your understanding of wisdom will be unchallenged. For those who seek, diligently continue until the experience sheds light upon the truth.

In this, you would have gained the knowledge of whether your efforts, focus and time, were worth the journey; such is the essence of wisdom. With this said, do what has been given you to do upon your time on this earth.

Remember it's not about what the world thinks you to be but rather who God created you to become in the time of distractions.

Colossians 2:8

"Beware lest any man spoil you through philosophy and vain deceit, after the tradition of men, after the rudiments of the world, and not after Christ."

- King James Version

12 CHAPTER

BALANCE OF THE MIND

The war has already been won, good has triumph over evil and the will of man still exist, as the gift which otherwise brings judgment upon the completion of one's journey. Out of sight out of mind is the fine line of between those who blindly seek and others who blindly follow. What is left within one's purpose, if knowledge is acquired to corrupt that which is truth upon the world?

This is where the balance of mind, reveals the direction of a journey we must all at some point traverse. This balance is in all that we do, think and feel within the boundaries of the world but is there more to this story. What do we really know about ourselves, about life and ultimately our created purposes?

Do we just scamper around throughout the ups and downs of life, hoping to feel inspired? Secretly desiring to be swept away by some supernatural force of greater understanding? Hoping to abandon the exhaust of spiritual responsibility by way of lack?

We in fact want to be free of the persecution of thought, questioning of one's choices and even truth within our embedded purposes. This mental quagmire is the very essence of what is meant by "the blind leading the blind."

In this is the fear of responsibility, even if the purpose of matter is for the fulfillment of life. For some reason, mankind still scampers around trying to find what has not been given but rather, search for the corrupted creations wield by his own hands.

Foolish in the intent to change the law of the land but within the will of mankind, something in the likelihood of power does come to fruition. This is nothing more than denial. Only when this desperate act of avoidance becomes seeded, spiritual influence is abruptly put on hold.

In this, the weeds of deceit will grow dense in the mind, shifting the balance between body, mind and soul and ultimately wreaking havoc on ones destined path.

Where does one go from here? When the idea or image of one's life isn't going as planned, it's mostly do to the cluttered vision of the mind.

The falsities of the mind can betray a person every time by way of results from actions taken. In this, if an idea created from a clouded mind is forced into reality, the evidence of such thinking will be the profound consequence.

At this point, if the circumstance becomes overwhelming, a much needed change can be implemented to balance the scale of one's path.

This is where the human potential embedded within the subconsciousness can be drawn upon.

No matter how deep the tipping scale of life is at any point, change can take place revealing remarkable blessings and spiritual stature; swiftly balancing ones troubled mind.

In this balance is when knowledge can supersede a person's circumstance, leveling out ones understanding of purpose. Moreover, lending to the pouring of a solid foundation, creating a base in which to stand firm and build upon one's strength, knowledge and ultimately the acquisition of wisdom.

This is good news to the unaware but for those of premeditated intent, those that are with selfish intent until the time to pay comes to pass, will not have the same fallback. In other words, their foundation will be weak upon construction and will suffer a harshly until balance is restored.

A reminder to the wise, the balance in which I speak, is in terms of the reality we create. This created reality goes back into the subject of our perceptions of life.

If one seeks the power of corruption within this life at the expense of others, then powerless one will become in actuality; that is in the forevermore of subconsciousness.

As referenced from THE CONSCIOUSNESS of MAN, what we do in this life, vastly affects the outcome in the realm of actuality; which of course is the eternal.

So in the blessed responsibility of my calling, allow me to open up and speak freely regarding one's true purpose. By now to have gotten this far in this book, you may be wondering how this all applies to your life.

Are you reading out of respect or politeness? Or are you truly looking to reveal within the pages what it requires to become the best version of yourself.

If this is what is expected, then you must first come to terms with who God created you to be in this life. Think about it, you were not created to "get all you can get" out of the spoils of the world and fade away into nothingness.

We were not blessed with the power of will, consciousness or love, just to vicariously go through life over-indulging in the temptations of the flesh. This is why all was given a certain amount of intuition, a certain spark and intuitive thrive to do something of importance within the timeframe of our existence.

The only problem with this process is, the acceptance of the world's perspective. With this comes the selfishness of personal lust, conjoined with the thought plan that there is power to be gained, money to be earn and perceptions to be created.

In this, money power and respect becomes the goal of the masses, far from what God intended mankind to have as a life of fulfillment.

So How do we get on track? It is my hope to write, speak or live by example in such a way, I can remind people that following the word of God is what's needed.

Here's something most fail to consider, finding wisdom is to find the peace in all matters.

Its represents the knowledge and know-how to flourish in life, making light of crippling situations and go forth to a higher understandings.

It requires humbleness in the likeness of failure, faith in a time of worry and maturity when responsibility is at its height of burden.

Wisdom doesn't sound so enticing when the light of day is shed upon its true purpose but what would life be without the comfort wisdom?

Fortunately this is a question we don't have to ponder for long, being we've either obtained a sense of wisdom or not. Why? Because true wisdom is of the Holy Spirit and this is an eternal a part of God.

Nothing we do as humans can replace God's purpose, plan or promise but what we 'can' do, is effect how we fit in his masterplan. So why not obtain wisdom for the betterment of life, freeing us from the bondage of spiritual confusions and darkness.

Again, just some quick reminders, please try and refrain from "buying" into someone else's ideas for your life. Don't be so quick to have another's thoughts change what's embedded in your heart, especially when you know it's your calling.

Why not accept the glory of our heavenly father's plan, to share upon the world as the light of his children? Continue to search for what is in your spirit and not in the likeness of others opinions.

Keep the faith in God's favor over your purpose and the lives of others in need, in this you will position yourself to receive all that is conducive from the wisdom gained.

When it comes to finding one's true self through mindfulness, enlightenment or the law of attraction, lean your heart to the teachings of Christ. Do this rather than following today's modern guru's masterplan for your happiness.

Let no man's carefully constructed, mass-blueprinted steps for a successful life, be sold unto you for your destiny's sake. Let no man's opinion be prescribed as your salvation nor convince you otherwise, that you are not God's perfect creation already.

Ask yourself how many self help books, diets and cheats does one need to actually feel good about their circumstances in life? No wonder the world of entrepreneurship, masterclasses and self-help gurus are endlessly abundant.

All one needs is to convince the masses that peace can be found without the consequences of spiritual order. Put on a thousand dollar suit, create personal content of one's luxury, confidence and expertise and wha-la! The promise of giving the answers to life's biggest challenges or desires.

This basically boils down to how to become a millionaire, enlightened beyond all practical means or abundant in all the ways the universe has to offer. But wait, there's more! All one has to do is click and save their seat by enrolling on the email list of the content providers webpage.

In this, at least be sure to learn with a greater goal in mind. So when making these choices, try and get spiritual confirmation that the program, masterclass or training is of an anointed, positive bible based structure.

I'm not trying to throw daggers at another's plan of business or life's goal but are we looking for answers to become leaders or leaders to declare us as followers? Are we in search of a better life or the comfortability of one's personal temptations, scattered amongst the distractions of the world?

Just know you're calling is spoken aloud within the eternal spirit of your subconscious.

Your purpose is written upon the chambers of your heart, awaiting your remembrance. Your mindfulness, that is the fullness of peace within the mind, can only be achieved by the living word of God within his forgiveness and mercy.

If you seek wisdom, then you must be prepared for the power, patience and knowledge that it provides.

This can only be obtained by the good of spirit, the sacrifice of one's idol thoughts and the humbleness to be a servant of God. Any other way of achievement, would be an act of denial and a total waste of time here on earth.

Know that your peace, purpose and destiny comes without a physical price tag! Christ has already ransomed himself, paid in full and laid the foundation for your eternal salvation.

Walk upon this soil, enrich the garden within your temple with the seed of Christ's teachings.

In this you will flourish and become connected within the body of Christ; readily available to receive that of wisdom sought after.

Again, when it comes to finding one's true self through mindfulness, enlightenment or any other means, no one needs to tell you to stop, slow down or meditate. Why? Because you already know how to pray. No one needs to sell, tell or convince you who you are, when you're fully capable of finding one's self in Christ.

The truth in the matter is, people will pay, follow and subscribe to whatever is easily obtainable, for the comfortability or achievement of their personal growth. Only issue derived from this way of goal oriented thinking is, it falls short of one's God given potential.

For example, you can enjoy a glass of your favorite beverage to help ease you into a relaxing night's sleep.

You can enjoy a movie that'll temporarily take your mind off the stressors within society, sending you upon a journey of intrigue and adventure.

Surely there is nothing wrong with investing in self help books, seminars or the like thereof to help guide you through the circumstances of concern but in all, these are examples of the temporary. Just know that self created issues are known to slow or agitate your progress, it's a part of life.

Only when It comes to that of eternity, God and his purpose for your creation, that's a whole new story and a matter of serious understanding.

This is why I offer my contribution as a course correction to those who might have fallen off course, just beginning their journey or confirming, that knowledge comes from many different often unlikely sources.

Even with the constant bombardment of distractions within and around our environment, at this stage in our lives we should know better. We should know to a certain extent what is required but the question is, do we really want to be who we were created to be?

I pose this question in light of searching for wisdom within the pages of this book.

In this case, wisdom will only be reflected upon the eyes of the honest, being you will no doubt receive what your perceptions allow as truth. If this is you, go forth and be amazed upon your walk.

Go and rely upon the embedment of purpose within your spirit and confidently lead by way of blessed example.

Do this in remembrance that someone already walked a painful path for you to be free. Someone bled upon the cross as the ultimate sacrifice for the eternity of your spirit and this spectacular someone rose again, ascending into heaven with your best interest of life at heart. This to one day, upon your diligent search be reunited with the comforter, allowing for you to become one within the wisdom of the Holy Spirit.

Remember, upon this journey if you decide to "not forgive" yourself or another because of the dismal understandings of your purpose, you in turn prevent the flow of wisdom to nourish within your mind.

In this know, you have the power of God in your hands and in your favor. Open up, being Christ has done the same for you and your eternal spirit.

1 Corinthians 2:9

"But as it is written, Eye hath not seen, nor ear heard, neither have entered into the heart of man, the things which God hath prepared for them that love him."

- Kings James Version

CHAPTER 13

MASTERY OF THOUGHT

Please understand, the descriptive meaning of the word wisdom holds many different perceptions and understandings. This is based from those of experienced knowledge, cultural backgrounds and spiritual convictions. All in some part regarding on how to live life, avoid the wiles of evils and why it's important to honor the word of God.

Nevertheless, at a minimum remember to encompass and empower these next few words, "The fear of the lord is the beginning of wisdom!" Proverbs 9:10

With this said, you will not be able to acquire the true power of wisdom, without first becoming humble and obedient to God's written word. In addition to this understanding, recall words are just words unless they hold beneficial meaning.

If not, the true root of the word will be misunderstood and soon lost overtime; making difficult its spiritual composition for future minds.

This is why a meek understanding, paired with a sense of humility towards the ancient knowledge of study, is so vastly important towards one's journey.

Holding on to this thought, I'll provide an example of how not fully understanding the depth of impact words can carry; ultimately affecting one's personal development. Although you've just recently read these next few words or are already familiar with them from the bible, let's take a deeper look into its meanings, again for the humility of learnings sake. "The fear of the lord is the beginning of wisdom!" Proverbs 9:10

This fear of which is spoken, speaks on two different levels of consciousness. First, for the followers of Christ and all that is good, "fear" in this meaning is to have reverence for the lord thy God.

Not to be scared of what he can do to you but rather respect and to never forget the blessings, show of mercy and favor he's given unto us all.

To fear in this sense, is to not forget and be thankful. This is why it is written "to fear the lord is the beginning of wisdom." It enters your mind into the receiving mode of God's will and mercy.

In other words, shed your light on the healthy fears of God, we practice this in our everyday mainstream of life anyway right?

What do we do when we fear losing our jobs? We work honest, more effective and attentive.

Some physically work harder on the job, making themselves more valuable, dependable and knowledgeable. Some go back to school and enhance their minds to be more suitable, staying ahead of the industrial curve.

Why? Because the possibility of one suddenly losing their financial stability, their insurance, paid vacation leave, sick days, retirement and all that comes with the security of having a good job is a fear we've created, whether most want to believe it or not.

On another scale, what if I had no respect or fear of the road while speed driving for excitement sake.

The repercussions of my causing a car accident due to speeding is not worth the "fear" of going to jail, causing someone or myself injury or even just getting a ticket. It's not healthy for me to fear any of the aforementioned scenarios, being it'll only bring on stress and anxiety.

This form of "fear" will in return cause sickness and disease to develop within the body. On the other hand accidents in life happen, so I've developed the healthy fear of respecting time and the speed limit while driving, investing in quality road insurance and driving with a specific goal in mind.

I'm thinking heaven is a pretty good goal. Christ is excellent insurance and having a healthy respect for God's limits and time for my life on earth puts me in good hands.

This was not a pun or plug for "the good hands" of All State Insurance but I hear their very reliable!

Getting back on track, yes, there are other jobs for equal or even higher wages but there's only one God and his benefit package outweighs any other! Best to fear the lord in the sense that all is well in his eyes for your eternal life sake. Turning your back on this understanding will put you in the other group of fear, that is the doers of denial.

In this concept, they within their own consciousness creates the fear of punishment, death and hell! Even though Christ has died and rose again to wipe their slate clean!

This on a much simpler scale is like siblings getting in trouble at school and upon the fear of the fathers punishment, chooses to freeze outside in the cold of winter, then to allow the warmth of mother to let them in!

Think about it, people are actually sending themselves to hell without the help of the devil, by way of their own perceived consciousness in fear.

This is why I and others of blessed content say something to the likelihood of "change your perception of the world and the world or the like thereof will change as well."

Now let's start by deciphering the subtitle of this book, the Age of Mindfulness. It was my goal to choose such a title within the absolute faith, that I would remind those caught up in the deceit of times to slow down. More specifically, those seemingly hellbent on eradicating personal development, within the principles of the living word of God.

This to first and foremost try and fully understand what's actually going on in their heads, regarding truth as opposed to the wiles of deceit. In this comes full circle as to the importance to change our perceptions from sensationalism, to that of mental clarity.

Bam! There it is! The underlying purpose of those of higher consciousness to speak, sing, lead or commit to literature, a path back to the truth of matter; that is the Holy Bible. Any art form used to tell a story or lead by positive example as a light for God's glory, is the reason we must continue to work on our embedded craft, furthermore sharing his wisdom.

Currently in today's society, there has been an unprecedented movement pushing unmerited philosophies and new concepts, geared towards a myriad of new biblical conceptions.

That is, purposely camouflaged under the perception of cool ideas, movie analogies and feel good opinions. In this the youth and unaware of our generation, will unknowingly be blinded within a battle they could not possibly fathom.

This all to pair up and confuse historical references, in hopes of creating new or certain thought patterns for our up and coming leaders of spiritual wealth.

Know that the deceit starts by first getting people to accept themselves for who they are and the actions they choose; seems innocent enough.

Then on to the revelation that their truth, is all that matters per they're morally opinionated sakes. Soon after falling into groups of like-minded thinking, they eventually fall through the cracks of the overall intent of deceit.

Now they're broken and ready to believe anything resembling peace of higher understanding. Enter in "you are Gods!" and "the law of attraction" and suddenly the masses believes all can escape the atrocities of the world within their mindfulness! This with the seeded purpose of ideas, opinions and thought processes, centered specifically on manipulating one's cognitive ability to accept selfishness as the norm.

In this, making light of the means to cope with the stressors created within the life process. This as a chosen path, opposed to understanding the truths within the world.

Again, there has been a perpetuated shift in consciousness, targeting the complacency of man's will. In this, saturating the heart of mankind's perception, simultaneously drowning in the idolization of one's personal desires.

We must find the root of solitude but not from our own tainted means of consciousness. This search will require the clarity found through personal faith and commitment.

In this, we shall bend to the knee of our minds and up-root the meanings of things buried under the false perceptions of ill will; let us begin.

Let's start by looking at the word age, what comes to mind? The age of a fine wine from the vineyards of California, the seasoned perfection of dry aged beef to the liking of a professional chef or does the image of age, exploit the numerical value of ones years in life?

The answer depends on the readers ability to associate the words meanings, within the personal experiences shared upon their journey.

In this case, maybe the lovely editor of this book Laura Garfield, has a deep appreciation for aroma casted from the crystal glass of a skillfully aged red wine.

What about my culinary experience as a professional chef, indulging in the smokiness of an aged cut of New York strip, char seared on the grill with just a hint of garlic peppercorn.

Now how about the age of mindfulness as in the subtitle of this book? What does it mean to you?

Here's what I'd like you to see. Age is of no concern to God's' plan being he's eternal.

In this, the only people thinking of "age," are those who experience it through the various levels and values of their lives. This is why understanding the root word is important, especially if one looks to utilize   the set compilations of words for guidance.

As for "the Age of Mindfulness,"I wanted to center on the understanding that we are in an age of carefully constructed distractions. In other words an elongated-fad of sorts,   purposely seeding todays mindset with destructive distractions.

    Which is why I offer a course correction by way of 'THE BOOK of KNOWLEDGE,'' to assist in ones search. With this said, it is my faith to remind people that finding oneself is not sealed within the wallets of the entrepreneur, the guru's of meditation or the new found speakers of universal laws.

In this, reminding and uniting the seekers of peace, to bring light through Christ's examples. Further reminding those in need, that the knowledge of self-fulfillment already exist within the chambers of a purified heart. This well noted within the word of God throughout the scriptures of the Holy Bible.

Let's look at the word mind, from the broken word mindfulness. Without doubt one of the buzzwords of the century, we hear it all the time, finding mindfulness in one-self. Just what does that actually mean?

Most people prescribe that it means finding peace from within but in actually, it means the blocking out the externally deemed worrisome.

Makes sense at first but again, when you start to look closer to the words and how it applies to you life, you may find yourself at a loss. For instance, when you think of mind what do you think?

Can you associate your experience with the mind, the same way another could with associate with other tangible things in life such as the fine wine spoken to earlier?

Understand the mind is a far more difficult to comprehend being the mind doesn't have form, although by way of being aware we know it exists.

For those who believe the mind is the brain and with this we can study on an anatomical level, let me enlighten the unnecessary burden of this cluttered way of thinking. I'll provide the short version, as stay on track with the purpose of this book.

The brain is a biological part of the human body, used for the physical motor functions and operations to navigate, reproduce and communicate within this reality.

It's filled with neurons which are transmitters within our nervous system for sending information back and forth through the nerve cells of muscles, glands and all that is required for the successful achievement of staying alive.

When It comes to the mind, well that's an entirely different subject. Although I do believe within the subconscious part of our spirit, there relies an unimaginable amount of power and control over our mind, body and soul but we tend to have a disconnect with this source.

I believe it has a lot to do with the signals, waves or vibrations transmitting through the channels of our faith, our spiritual connection with God and of course the endless wonders within the faculties of our minds. Which leads us back to the difference between the brain and the mind.

Simply put, the brain is a biological electrical component used to assist the body's physical ability, the mind is more of a transmitting radio station, equipped with powerful antennas used for receiving and transmitting information through that which extends beyond our reality.

With this said, I'd like to touch quickly on the subject of the neuron again, being it seems to have great implications regarding the sharing of information.

When considering the brain and it's transmitting abilities, we were raised to focus solely on the image of the brain at times.

As mentioned before, when we tend to concentrate, we often bow are heads or place our finger on our temples as to assist the concentration.

If this helps you, there's nothing wrong with what works for you but allow me to add a bit more understanding. With regards of the transmitting of neurons in the brain, there are also millions upon millions located in the heart as well as the gut.

This may help your understanding more when you say "I had a gut feeling" ... or "my gut was telling me to ..." and not to forget "I had a feeling in my heart to open up and give." Maybe what you think and feel comes from more than just your brain.

Maybe what you think and feel comes more from the collaboration of your body. In this, composed of the connecting transmitters throughout the complete anatomical structure we call the physical temple.

This has nothing to do with finding oneself, being the subconscious handles this department on its own.

Even though words have power, they can become more powerful when spoken within the inspiration of one's heart. This entails why it's so vitally important to reverence the teachings of the word of God.

Understanding the fear of the lord in respect to our purpose in life as well as eternally, takes the manifestation of wickedness within the heart and transforms it anew. This allows for the beginning of knowledge to flow like a fountain through the chambers of your heart.

Upon this, the tongue is sweet with the nectar of God's intent, balanced precisely within the words you speak. Powerful your words are, flourishing upon your destined path. With this experience, one can now use the wisdom gained to discern the goodness within the meaning of life.

In the matters of life, everyday choices will bring about the pondering of many circumstances, whether of ease or not. Know that one of wisdom, will possess the ability of character to lead by spiritual example; this as opposed to suffering the consequences of wicked decisions.

Again, know that if man tries to acquire wisdom, in such a manner as to do evil upon the world, the bitter tongue of his deceit will fail upon closed ears; expediting his journey towards damnation.

With this said, allow me to add by way of spiritual instruction the ten commandments from the King James Bible.

What other way to prepare for the anointing of wisdom, than to be reminded the blueprint of God's success for our journey upon the earth.

Know that a balance between good and evil is still ever present within the world we live in, being the human condition summits to such battle. As stated earlier within the chapters "the war has already been won." What we're fighting today is the accepted battle of the mind, that is struggling with the temptations of the flesh.

The much larger picture is that of our eternal spirits and being Christ has given us a "get out of hell pass," we have all that's required to make it into the kingdom.

Moreover, the only issue that could prevent this spiritually destined path, is our own created will to fail. That is the submission of one's guilt or fears, even the denial of what is known to be right, within one's blessed purpose in life.

Again, God gave us will but for the blessed oppositions of choices he knew we'd make. As such, the consequences from our mistakes, should cause us to see the goodness in God's original plan for our lives.

Thus the platform, the balance and what is famously written as the Ten Commandments is shared within the pages of this book. This goes without saying "how can a book on wisdom, not include the foundation of his commandments."

Simple as it may appear, it's a set foundation of rules, that extended knowledge far beyond what was once broken upon the ears of the deaf.

Take some time and recite this as you walk with the mindset of spiritual acquisition and remember, all that is created for you will soon come to pass.

THE TEN COMMANDMENTS

King James Version

Thou shalt have no other gods before me.

Thou shalt not make unto thee any graven image, or any likeness of any thing that is in heaven above, or that is in the earth beneath, or that is in the water under the earth.

Thou shalt not bow down thyself to them, nor serve them: for I the Lord thy God am a jealous God, visiting the iniquity of the fathers upon the children unto the third and fourth generation of them that hate me; And shewing mercy unto thousands of them that love me, and keep my commandments.

Thou shalt not take the name of the Lord thy God in vain; for the Lord will not hold him guiltless that taketh his name in vain.

Remember the sabbath day, to keep it holy. Six days shalt thou labour, and do all thy work: But the seventh day is the sabbath of the Lord thy God: in it thou shalt not do any work, thou, nor thy son, nor thy daughter, thy manservant, nor thy maidservant, nor thy cattle, nor thy stranger that is within thy gates:

For in six days the Lord made heaven and earth, the sea, and all that in them is, and rested the seventh day: wherefore the Lord blessed the sabbath day, and hallowed it.

Honor thy father and thy mother: that thy days may be long upon the land which the Lord thy God giveth thee.

Thou shalt not kill.

Thou shalt not commit adultery.

Thou shalt not steal.

Thou shalt not bear false witness against thy neighbor.

Thou shalt not covet thy neighbor's house, thou shalt not covet thy neighbor's wife, nor his manservant, nor his maidservant, nor his ox, nor his ass, nor any thing that is thy neighbor's. (KJV)

Notice how some words over time stand out, often creating different images or understandings? Let this not persuade your thought process, other than wanting to seek the root of the word or meanings in full.

Know that to seek wisdom not only requires faith but repentance and obedience to the word of God. In this you will stay strengthened upon your journey.

If weakness troubles your mind, exercise your trust in purpose, kneel in prayer and keep in faith that all is awaiting within your created purpose.

Travel well within this life, seek what has been given unto you and praise in advance. Your blessed destiny is soon coming into fruition, so be prepare; God bless your journey.

Personal Note:

As the author of this book, I hold the blessed responsibility of teaching, sharing and giving in total honesty; it is truly a privilege and I thank you for taking part in this journey.

Know that as a man of God, I am and will always be his servant, readily available to serve, rapport and connect with you as we are the body of Christ in ministry. May God continue to bless and bestow favor upon your journey.

The truth in wisdom is never ending, so in the completion of THE BOOK of WISDOM: the age of mindfulness; I'll leave it where it all began.

Genesis 1:3

"In the beginning God created the heaven and the earth. And the earth was without form, and void; and darkness was upon the face of the deep. And the Spirit of God moved upon the face of the waters. And God said, Let there be light: and there was light. And God saw the light, that it was good: and God divided the light from the darkness." - King James Bible.

Thank you.

GET TO KNOW THE AUTHOR

Q&A's for Reginald O'Neal Gibson

What is you're previous book THE CONSCIOUS-NESS of MAN about?

This book is the seed of my journey, deeply rooted within the soil of my purpose since childhood. Giving rise to confirmations as well as spiritual leadership to a generation in search of wisdom.

It clarifies for others, how I became reunited with my purpose as a humble servant of God. In this, THE CONSCIOUSNESS of MAN witnesses the similarities of our journeys and how it reflects mankind's mental perceptions, ideas and opinions in today's societal zeitgeist.

How does your writing contribute or serve within the book community or world thereof, being there are so many books flooding the market on self help?

My writing serves as the progression of man's inner need, potential and purpose to share experiences, knowledge and beliefs for the continuation of betterment by truth.

In other words, help to pass down knowledge that will strengthen mankind's purpose in life. Simply put, getting back to the word of God, as a blueprint or basis of our everyday survival.

Do you have a background in psychology, neurology or theology?

We all have a background of understanding to a certain degree, in respect to the experiences of human existence. If you're asking, if I'm and expert on the topics of psychology, neurology or theology, the answer would be "not in the least" but neither does any human being walking on this planet.

Not in the sense we've come to believe what "the experts" are truly about. An "expert" relating to the definition of acquiring authoritative or comprehensive knowledge on a matter of particularity simply means, one who has studied groups and literature of collected data and researched in and of a certain time span, that could show patterns and possibilities.

This in no way means that an expert on sleep patterns, "knows all" about the resting process or purpose. Moreover, has a pretty good assumption or understanding based off statistical analysis derived from controlled studies.

Know that life is a process of continuous change and development and one of many things we know, is that with change comes new information.

Thus the best we have are acronyms of specified studies, concerning data, research and a number of hours credited as the experience accumulated to create our best assumptions, conclusions or understandings.

For example, a field expert called to witness in a court of law within a certain positive regard, will be offset by an opposing expert of negative regard. This concerning the same topic of interest, just perceived differently.

With this said, the only truth to be discovered, is that one truly knows nothing at all in it's entirely but is always open to the revelation of truth.

In regard to a court of law and opposing experts, what hangs in the balance maybe ones freedom.

In the end after both experts in specified fields gave their depositions, the judge relies on his understandings of current law paired with the jurors who offers their best assumptions, based off the persuasion of the experts!

Point is, it's not about being an expert to convince but rather being honest in knowing thy self, while sharing the wisdom of blessed experiences to help and confirm with others; that's why this book was written.

Again, not to persuade or coerce but to confirm upon communion that we are truly one within God's purpose.

With that said, If I had to choose I'd lean more to the professional or someone of specified studies, before I'd trust someone's idealistic opinions driven by personal means or agenda.

Often I follow and research the consistency and relevancy on new discoveries within science, physics and theology, as it pertains to the human experience.

Moreover, the essence of my background is mastery of self, that of true diligence with a stern commitment to finding, understanding and relating to the human potential and purpose as it pertains to God's master plan for mankind.

I acknowledge the importance and need of the experts in the specialized fields relating to medical science, psychology and theology but again, my authority derives from knowing truth of self by way of experience, spiritual enlightenment and communion within the Holy Spirit.

In this, there is no standardized testing, degree of completion or monetized acronym added to my birth name but rather the results of my actions, successes and God given purpose.

Will I pursue specialized education in certain fields of expertise; yes. I'm currently doing so but only for the clarity of a world seeking credential before voice.

Whatever it takes to help lead people back to God's original design for our purpose, abundance and happiness. But know that all the credentials, degrees and specialized acronyms means nothing upon the day God calls us home.

Which is why my "expertise," is that of fulfilling my calling by way of the Holy Spirit in Jesus name.

In some of your written works, you've added a "HIDDEN CHAPTER," please explain why?

When I include a "Hidden Chapter" in my books, it's only because I was spiritually influenced to go deeper within the transparency of my heart.

In this, most often I'd reveal a vision, circumstance or blessing so powerful, that it was one of many key factors that course corrected my direction in life, either through enlightenment, thought process or physical change.

What is THE BOOK of WISDOM: The Age of Mindfulness really about?

As mentioned in a previous answer, "often I follow and research the consistency and relevancy on new discoveries within science, physics and theology."

In this, If I'm spiritually convinced that a balance needs to be ushered in, I add my take on the matter as with many who are anointed to speak in truth.

More specifically, this book is about reminding those who seek the passive or easy way of hard to digest principles, not to be mislead by wicked intentions.

For example, to seek mindfulness in the mindset of a cluttered mind is a fallacy. One must clear their minds not for self idolization but for all that is good in this world; with this said peace can be found.

How will the knowledge expressed in this book, help or guide others within their everyday routines of life?

The transparency in which I write, express and share knowledge will without fail, strike an accord with others by way of confirmation and comparison to their journeys as well. In this giving hope to others still struggling through, about to go through or coming out of the trials within life.

My humbled knowledge expressed will assist others within the battlefields of their minds, giving rise to confidence, clarity and purpose.

Where did you obtain the knowledge or inspiration to write this/these books?

The majority of knowledge obtained came from my spiritual guidance through childhood experience until present.

The ups and downs, successes and failures with the addition of a life filled with spiritual teachings through biblical reference and gained wisdom along the journey.

Still today at any given time, knowledge, clarity and visions are released in increments per trials encountered throughout my life.

This is true amongst us all, being we've been embedded with wisdom written upon the chambers of our hearts.

Who is your mentor, inspiration or leader by example?

I have no singular mentor other than the shared wisdom of the Holy Spirit. In other words, I acquire knowledge from my dreams, visions and the living word of God. With this said, I acknowledge and acquire various meanings, understandings and principles collectively from the journeys of others tribulations and successes in life.

More over, along this journey in life I've acquired the ability to absorb truth in the matter of denial, discernment in the face of iniquity and peace, within the false perceptions of a cluttered world; mind, body and soul.

When it comes to inspirations, know that when peace dwells within your heart, all forms on any level of God's creation can be of great influence and importance.

With this said, there are speakers of today, men and women of God, ministers and authors past and present that in someway reminded, hinted or confirmed what I've been lead to believe since birth.

Some of their names are household, others maybe not so much but all, even yourself are an intricate part of God's overall purpose of positive information sharing.

Notable mentions such as Dr. Miles Monroe, William Franklin Graham Jr., Norman Vincent Peale, Zig Ziglar, Dr. Martin Luther King, Earl Nightingale, Less Brown, Jim Rhon, Lisa Nichols, Napoleon Hill and Eric Thomas.

These just to name a few, struck my attention along the journey of conformational awareness, further reminding me I wasn't alone open the path of the righteous.

Know that there are others as well, not so widely known but still a powerful force when the Holy Spirit moves through their purpose of heart. One such person is Mr. Robert Lewis Parker of Columbus, Ohio.

I crossed paths with this God fearing man and I must say the conversations we've shared on many occasions were truly of God's purpose.

You'll never know when a course correction of focus will come your way but when it does, you'll know by the overwhelming anointing of the Holy Spirit, either in you or from another source.

In this is why I mentioned the name of Mr. Parker, his laughter, his smile and his songs of praise on the days of good and bad reminded me, that any day of breath in our lungs are a given day by God, worthy of his praise and worship.

What authors do you follow or aspire to be like?

I do not follow any authors but I do acknowledge an author's dedication, passion and purpose to a great degree. Furthermore, I'm not going to name drop another's notability for my brand or personal gain.

Honestly, I believe every author should have their own personal style of writing, inspiration or vision. If not, are they really who they say they are or are they merely the collective inspirations of another's rewritten authoritative literature?

Think about it. Being I primarily focus on my spiritual convictions as well as personal experiences, I'm not driven to be influenced by another's perception, idea or opinions. At least not until I get my thoughts, feelings and stories fully out. Afterwards, I can confirm and communion with others along the journey.

What I do follow is national trends of persuasive personal development. In this I research patterns of media influenced propaganda regarding past, present and future understandings.

More often than none, the results of my research turns out to be more than just a coincidence. Meaning it often pans out to be shrewd insinuations geared towards alternate perceptions in the teachings of biblical principles. Specifically on matters pertaining to historical importance, sponsored opinions and or "the powers that be."

For example, I like to research and follow, how current trends paraphrases the word of God within the Holy Bible. When this happens, corruption within the principalities will manipulate the passiveness of human potential for their personal gain.

In this, is why I'm spiritually convicted to help balance what is needed, for those who seek guidance along the righteous path of their journey.

There is so much cluttered and misconstrued information purposely being shoveled out into the world, I just want to do my part in leading people back to the origins of truth. Furthermore, alleviating the weight of conscious overload burdened upon our minds.

To be continued, thank you.

A LITTLE BACKGROUND ABOUT YOUR AUTHOR

(Excerpt from his website zoeylifesite.com)

Here's a little something personal about the man God created in me. For those who "kinda" know me, either through my work, acquaintance of my wife or even online presence. Know that most people accept others solely by the character they display or the result of their actions.

For the most part, this is the best we can do. The majority often assume, become judgmental or simply fall into speculation (I was like this once upon a time).

This being it's far more comfortable to view someone else's life, through one's own opinions, understandings and even moral values.

Simply put, when it comes to interpersonal communications, some people may not have developed the skill level to really listen, (mainly men from what I've been told) nor have they developed the patience to share empathy or even ask questions in honest regard; especially at the beginning of another's relationship.

People consisting of family and friends often for the purposes of (polite gossip), unmerited curiosities or just plain playing the devil's advocate, try to fit in their own understanding or picture. Thus, choosing to fit the pieces of their own puzzled mind into their reality.

So in this mindset and years later, I'd like to offer a bit more about who I am, what I claim my purposes to be and what makes me tick/think or react, in the manner of a leader by example. This gets a little personal being at one point in my life, it was considered to be embarrassing but such is life; if lived right.

My upbringing like many was not the greatest but was blessed beyond my years of youthful understanding. Moreover, I grew up hard, rigid and continuously hurt.

In my teen years I became overly protective, closed off and blinded to the goodness in life.

My early adult years were of anger and oppression but fortunately I found solitude, with a numbing-physical strength I came to fall in love with (called fighting). By this time in my life, my body was scarred with bullets and knife wounds, my hands and knuckles were callused, leathery and always clenched.

My eyes only seen the darkness of the world, as I constantly prepared for the worse case scenario around every corner. Tangible goals held too closely only to crumble upon my feet, was just another day of expectancy.

I was always preparing for the next fight or like thereof, as the study of ninjutsu was my (or so I thought) Innate passion. I recall enduring hundreds of fist push ups on concrete and broken glass, shin kicking trees and mastering weapons of battle, just because it was feasible to my out-look on life.

I endured this act of insecurity and pain, until I became content with a lifestyle of misery and turmoil. After a while of this form of lustful denial, I started to enjoyed the sen-sation of pain whether mental or physical.

What could I say, being it was the only sensation my body could feel.

Rigid in the bliss of my ignorance, I felt I could no longer be hurt, challenged or even caught off guard, so pridefully I journeyed out into the world. Soon afterwards, I did something unlike the warrior I cherished within.

I took an unlikely turn at the flip of her hair, seemingly flowing "in slow motion," landing just right in the glimmer of light over her shoulder. At the time I didn't know what I was thinking! I knew it wasn't lust but more so of the spirit.

In short, I met my future wife Kelly! Completely oppo-site of what I'd thought a woman to be, she was strangely different. She was quirky, unimaginably lively and for some reason always glowing with smile. Nothing about her at-tracted me or so I thought, until her light entered the dark-ness of my dreams and corrupted understandings.

Now I was officially confused! Simultaneously the spirit that dwelt in me since childhood, started to speak louder and with more clarity, almost yelling within the thought process I've grown to adore.

"She is for you!" Over and over again "she is for you!" I tried to fight this thing but her exuberant personality taunted my ego to no end!

How could she see past my roughed, perfectly perfected "standoffish" ways! Her smile was almost as if I was missing out on something completely meant for my purpose.

On many occasions I tried to break this connection because I knew that in kelly's world the rain didn't exist but in my world, I welcomed the brute of the storm, hands raised high boldly playing in the drench of the cold, daring to be struck by lightning.

Why didn't she let me be? Why did the Holy Spirit wake me from the comfort of my nightmarish ways? At the time I didn't know but as I stand today, I fully understand that I was created not to be of the storm but to survive it, if and when it comes to pass.

Now growing within the created purpose of my life, I am whole. I am happy to say, I am alive in mind, body and spirit and to say the least it's absolutely amazing. My body has surprisingly regenerated in ways that even the doctors are astounded but I know this to be the workings of God.

It's as if the previous 20 years of hardship has somehow been magically erased.

All I know is, my wife Kelly is the beauty to my beast, the water that fills my cup to capacity and the God send that has change the very essence of my soul.

Now when people look at us, I'm sure someone or two (even in the kindness of their heart) still wonder a bit. That is, for those of inquisitive nature still trying to fit the pieces together, please rest assure. Kelly and I have a connection far stronger than physical lust, contentment or denial.

Simply put, Its spiritual on every positive level of human understanding. Moreover, as my children touch and pamper the scars, calluses and old wounds etched across my body, I've become even more-so filled with thankfulness and joy.

Now I can truly feel the sensations of care, love and innocence (with the occasional action figure impressed within the muscles of my back after a rough nights sleep). I can feel the warmth of my wife's gentle touch, as she pulls me in to cuddle.

Not to forget that seemingly immovable crumb, trapped under my bed sheet at night; such are the joys of being physically and mentally awaken from a mind bogglingly-nightmarish life.

Here's what I've learned, life can be so amazingly wonderful and understood, If we'd just open up and listen to the spirit of wisdom. Life can truly be filled with abundance, growth and overjoy. If we'd just/trust and get out of the way of our created insecurities, fears and judgments.

From what I gather, most people really don't know Kelly and I's story, but know that it's a story we all share to some degree.

If we'd all just change the perception of our lives and boldly choose love, faith and commitment over doubt. In this we'd easily find ourselves overcoming the storms, annoying crumbs and mind-numbing obstacles scattered within the world.

In conclusion, let us not stress over the missing pieces, seemingly lost from the big picture of our perceived understandings but rather continue on, until God's picture of our life is complete.

If you've asked yourself where's the WISDOM in this background story, good question! These last chapters are more so about a reflection going on in today's society. That is, a mirror image of what we've all at one point went through to become who we are; mostly by a either someone special or someone not.

Either way, ask yourself and be completely honest, are you the best expression of yourself or are you an expression of your past or present circumstances?

Know that both are a part of your mental and physical but only in the expression of learned wisdom can you identify your true purpose.

In other words, wisdom is derived from experience learned and utilized for the purposes of growth, progress and the positive continuation of life.

In my experience, I was lost in the mindset of my own perceived understandings but It took an outside force to cause me to seek the truth. Furthermore, with this truth there was clarity, in this clarity was peace and in this peace was the word of God; wisdom found.

James 1:15

*If any of you lack **wisdom**, let him ask of God, that giveth to all men liberally, and upbraideth not; and it shall be given him.

JOINT COMMITMENT

On this day of____/ ____/ ____, We willingly choose to uphold the quality of our created purpose's, by God's original intentions for our lives, in Jesus name; Amen.

_____

_____

_____

Name _____ Date___/___/___

Name _____ Date__/____/___

"Every day is a memory in the making, make it a good one."

– Reginald O'Neal Gibson

"The differences in people are not the issues of the world but rather, the indifference of knowledge shared."

- Reginald O'Neal Gibson

NOTES

_____

_____

_____

_____

_____

_____

_____

_____

_____

_____

Ecclesiastes 1:13

"And I gave my heart to seek and search out by wisdom concerning all things that are done under heaven: this sore travail hath God given to the sons of man to be exercised therewith."-King James Bible

"True wisdom is the mother of all knowledge, cultivated by past, present and future universal laws. Experienced and molded into unquestionable judgment, not to condemn or whether present understandings, but to uphold her call as the comforter. In this, the beauty and natural order of life is at hand. This freely opened for our needs, faith and desires upon the diligence of commitment."

-Reginald O'Neal Gibson

*THE BOOK of WISDOM: the age of mindfulness

by REGINALD O'NEAL GIBSON

Special Thanks

To these beautiful women of God's grace upon the world,
thank you for all that is your essence of life.

Linda Gibson-Taylor

Jackie Benjamin

Sharon M. Wartinger

Kelly Lynn Gibson

Jasmine J. Gibson

Jealisa L. Gibson

Adalynn Grace Gibson

Carolyn White

Kristin Thiel

Laura Garwood

Key points for discussion

1.) _____

2.) _____

3.) _____

4.) _____

5.) _____

6.) _____

7.) _____

THE BOOK OF WISDOM

"To all that seek truth, peace, wisdom and happiness, thank you for your time and consideration of my life's work upon your journey. Be blessed and always continue to seek, share and teach what God has given within your spirit. Together we can do our due diligence of good within the world. Again, may God continually bless your journey!"

-Reginald O'Neal Gibson

THE BOOK of WISDOM: the age of mindfulness

by REGINALD O'NEAL GIBSON

www.ingramcontent.com/pod-product-compliance
Lightning Source LLC
LaVergne TN
LVHW011156080426
835508LV00007B/428